D0419457

SCENES WE'D LIKE TO SEE

EWAN PHILLIPS, DAN PATTERSON, SIMON BULLIVANT, ROB COLLEY, DAN GASTER, GED PARSONS, GILES PILBROW, STEVE PUNT AND COLIN SWASH

B🌳XTREE

CONTENTS

1. UNSUCCESSFUL PERSONAL ADS

MEN SEEKING WOMEN / WOMEN SEEKING MEN

Me: short, hairy, fat, pigeon fancier. You: will probably already have moved on.

Ex-rugby player, dark, swarthy, square jawed, broad shouldered, 6' 3", hands like shovels, all woman.

Fun loving, wacky, crazy gal looking for man to share the good times, I'm mad me, all me friends say so, honest, I love you already I can tell, wooo arrrghhh waaaa.

Just back from extremely long time in foreign country. Looking for woman with low profile. Love children.

Hermaphrodite with flaming red hair, three beautiful legs, one eye, broken nose, no teeth seeks similar.

Widow, 56, likes opera and cinema. Seeks professional male for long country walks, candlelit dinners and eye-watering anal sex.

Companion required for long sessions of Sudoku. No timewasters.

Long-term gay man, looking to get back 'out there', no STDs, once bitten and all that.

Bride with six sisters seeks man from large family.

Calm down dear, this is just a personal ad.

Outspoken monoped, recently divorced, looking for ageing millionaire for long hops in the country.

Dull, unimaginative and unadventurous person seeks soulmate. Won't travel.

They said I should never be released, they said I am a danger to women, let's prove them wrong…

Me: curvy, great sense of humour, loves food, larger than life, positive, enjoys cooking, dining out, bubbly personality. You: Must like a fat lass.

Me: Man. You: Woman preferably.

Man with A.D.D. seeks woman for companionship, fun, long … ooh look, car for sale, £1,500!

Dastardly cad seeks lonely, wealthy spinster with understanding solicitor for exertion-filled final few months.

Straight man seeks comedian with jokes after death of funny half of double act.

Were you that man on the tube last week? I was that woman. Call me! Anon.

Caveman seeks match.

Man seeks man willing to kill and eat him or, if not, for theatre, days out in the country and pub quizzes.

Were you the blonde running fast on Hampstead Heath at 9.30 on Tuesday night? I was the man in the black balaclava running close behind. Wish we'd had chance to talk. Call me.

2. GREETINGS CARDS THAT WOULDN'T SELL (Part 1)

Good Luck To The Nicest Paedophile We've Ever Worked With

Now that you've lost your leg...

Congratulations on passing your STD test!

Hope your paper cut heals soon

Royal Wedding 10th Anniversary

To a fine set of grandparents: congratulations on your golden shower

Sorry about your face

Congratulations, you're Minister for Trade and Industry

Happy 12th birthday and congratulations on the birth of your second child

Happy Cloning to you and to you and to you

Sorry to hear you're a hate-filled cleric

Congratulations on putting the death of your first wife behind you, and remarrying

3. LINES YOU WOULDN'T FIND IN A HARRY POTTER BOOK (Part 1)

This is a true story.

'So you killed your own parents, Harry?'

'You were better than Ron,' said Harry as he withdrew from Hermione and lit a cigarette.

'My work here is done,' said Harry before flying away.

Hermione crawled from the rubble suffering from the effects of the bomb's radiation.

Mr and Mrs Potter didn't want Harry, so they dreamt up an incredible cover story to get rid of him ...

So, evil had triumphed.

'Death to the West!' shouted Voldemort as the flames licked Hogwarts.

'I like it here in the Shire,' said the Hobbit.

At last it dawned on Ron: with all his magic powers, he didn't have to be ginger any more.

And Harry begat Zorab ...

Harry Potter, the boy who never grew up thanks to a rare genetic condition ...

'You've only got one GCSE, Harry. What the bloody hell have you been doing for the last seven years?'

Logging on to YouTube, Harry watched the flickering images of fundamentalists finishing off Nearly Headless Nick ...

According to the *Daily Express*, first-time buyers like Hagrid are being priced out of the market.

The rafters creaked eerily as Harry's lifeless corpse swung to and fro on the end of a frayed noose. 'A classic case of too much, too young,' said Snape.

'Have you heard? The police have taken away Dumbledore's hard drive!'

'Have you noticed the resemblance between Hagrid and Robbie Coltrane?' asked Hermione.

'I've turned my cock into a frog!' Ron exclaimed.

It was Harry's eighteenth birthday, and he slipped on his Nazi uniform, ready for the party.

'Where's Ron?' asked Harry. 'He flew his broomstick into the engine of an F17,' said Hermione.

4. UNLIKELY CONCERTS

Britney Spears & Amy Winehouse
drink Magners and improvise

The Al-Qaeda Singers

Ann Widdecombe vs the Pussycat Dolls

Gordon Brown's 'Songs from the Shows'

Cherie Blair Unplugged

The Dreamers minus Freddie, a cappella

Heather Mills and Yoko Ono Sing the Beatles

Cliff Richard in Silent Prayer

Chesney Hawkes
My Fifty Greatest Hits

Michael Barrymore and Friends

Gerry Without his Pacemaker

St Winnifred's School Choir
Sing Napalm Death

Gary Glitter and the Minipops

Class 3C perform 'The Golden Hour
of Beginner's Recorder Classics'

The Rolling Stones
'This really is it this time'
tour

Kim Jong Il Sings
Shirley Bassey

5. LETTERS IGNORED BY 'JIM'LL FIX IT'

Dear Jim, I am a fifteen-year-old boy scout and am desperate to see a real-life pair of tits, what can I do?

Dear Jim, I am an unpopular African dictator and am about to have an election, could you fix it for me?

Dear Jim, could you fix it for me to see Amy Winehouse in concert? Love from all the people who bought tickets for her tour.

Dear Jim, can you fix it? I can, love Bob the Builder.

Dear Jim, can you kill Princess Diana and make it look like an accident? Love Phil and Liz, London.

Dear Jim, can you fix it for me to become a famous TV presenter despite having no obviously discernible talent and just a funny voice, odd hair, terrible dress-sense and a habit of smoking cigars constantly?

Hi Jim, our cat's a randy bastard – can you fix him?

Greetings Mr Jim'll, I am a Nigerian general with £20 million to deposit in your bank account ...

Hi Jim, I've got a lot of money riding on the 2.30 at Haydock. Can you fix it for me?

Dear Jim, now then now then, guys and gals, have a letter here, howzabout that then, ladies and gents, Dr Magic, very busy man, special chair, goodness gracious me, young lady, clunk-click, this is the age of the train, pop that badge on there like that, champ, Top of the Pops. Love from Jim there you see.

Dear Jim, I am a billionaire owner of a Premiership club that would love to win the Champions League. Can you fix it for me?

Dear Jim, I would like to spend some time in the company of a bizarre octogenarian and the wardrobe of his long-dead mother. Could you fix it for me?

Dear Jim, I am a footballer earning £55,000 a week and am convinced I am actually worth £90,000 at a rival London club. Can you fix it for me?

Dear Jim, my boiler has packed up – can you fix it?

Dear Jim, I was a cub scout featured on your programme in the 1980s, and due to a faulty seat belt have been strapped into a f*cking rollercoaster for the last twenty-six years. Can you fix it for me to be rescued?

Dear Jim, I have just won the football pools so I don't have to work answering the mail on your shit show any more.

6. UNLIKELY SMALL ADS (Part 1)

WANTED

Gullibility test kit – send £19.99 now!

Wedding dress for sale, size 36, unused – slight éclair stains on front.

Portfolio of shares for very quick sale. £500 o.n.o.

WANTED:
undroppable soap. Contact G. Glitter.

Tickets for Ben Elton musical – genuine reason for sale: it's shite.

WANTED:
swear box. Industrial size, min. 8 cubic metres. Apply G. F*cking Ramsay.

Condom for sale – slight tear. Rinse thoroughly.

Limited-edition 'Diana Crash' memorial plate for sale. Slightly chipped.

Holiday to Ayia Napa – price includes accommodation, food, drink and STD treatment.

NOT WANTED:
cleaner/housekeeper, apply Tracey Emin.

Suspiciouslycheaptickets.com – we fly you to within 200 miles of where you want to go.

LOST IN LONDON:
container of Polonium[210].
If found, please contact
Vlad on Moscow-312456.

FOR SALE:
Unwanted Christmas
present – one gold-plated
leg inscribed *To Heather
with Love*.

Nude painting of a young
Cherie Blair, make me an
offer, please.

Heir to the crown turning
sixty, seeks assassin for
urgent job.

Faintest clue required.
If you can help, contact
Alistair Darling.

SWF, GSOH seeks extra
vowels for good scrabble
score.

Technophobic? Simply
download our helpful
podcast at
www.technophobe.com

Box of finest Havana cigars
– slightly damp. Contact B.
Clinton.

Titanic memorabilia
– perfectly preserved
underwater. Buyer collects.

Radical imams required.
Must have GSOH and own
hook.

Injured at work? Want to
sue your boss? Then f**k off
to America.

Struggling with lots of small
debts? Why not consolidate
them into one impossibly
huge debt?

Stop snoring – fast! – with
this kitchen knife. Stab your
husband and say goodbye
to nocturnal rumble-misery
for ever!

FOR SALE:
one stick of dynamite, used.

7. UNPOPULAR COCKTAILS

The Long Slow Uncomfortable Screw Against a Wheelie Bin

Cup-a Sick (soup, cup, absinthe)

Bald Russian (tea, sushi, polonium^{210}, the KGB)

The Winehouse (gin, hair, heroin, coke, you name it and more gin)

Sex in an Alleyway (bucket of alcohol, holiday in Ibiza, Essex girl)

Overpriced Health Drink (a carrot, water, large bill)

On the Blob (moods, snaps, tantrums, appetite)

Low-Budget Holiday (uncooked meat, unwashed hands, rinse in water supply, add a dash to the toilet, can help weight loss)

The Almond Surprise (amyl nitrite, bucket of jizz, stomach pump)

The Exchange-Rate Mechanism (very dry gin, remove gin)

Phlegm Punch (turkey, Tamiflu, H5N1)

The Doherty (drugs, alcohol, junk food, shaken but won't stir)

The Prescott (lager, chips, brown sauce, chipolata, cocktail umbrella, don't worry if you haven't got the cocktail umbrella)

8. UNAPPETISING THINGS TO READ ON A MENU (Part 1)

Coq au man

Lightly toasted fillet of Jack Russell on a woodlouse celeriac

Testicles

The Not Really That Special

Board of cheeses (Dairylea, Cheese Strings, Laughing Cow, Primula and a selection of Wotsits)

Welcome to Gordon Banks at Claridge's

Weekly Specials:

MONDAY: *nothing*
TUESDAY: *nothing*
WEDNESDAY: *f*ck all*
THURSDAY: *chef can't be arsed*
FRIDAY: *an apple*
SATURDAY: *yeah right*
SUNDAY: *closed*

A 65% service charge will be added for your convenience
(We've added a further 20% to your bill as an added insult on top of the dreadful service)

9. BAD FIRST INTERVIEW QUESTIONS

'You were lucky to get a point there eh, Sir Alex?'

'What are your views on the tabloid press, Heather?'

'So I can get bird flu simply by doing this to this bird?'

'Jordan, can you just sing a bit of it for us now?'

'Could you drive me to where you were keeping the British journalist hostage?'

'Are you trying to seduce me, Miss Widdecombe?'

'Would you like something to drink first, Mr Kennedy?'

'Do you mind if I fart?'

'And for your first record, Mr bin Laden?'

'Do you mind if I take off my trousers?'

'Got any gear, Mr Cameron?'

'Do you swallow?'

'Wayne Rooney, in your opinion – *The Golden Notebook* excepted – does Doris Lessing's oeuvre truly merit a Nobel Prize?'

'Are you happy with a verdict of accidental death, Mr al Fayed?'

'Mrs Irwin . . . do you agree Steve was asking for it?'

'Kerry, have you got any coke on you?'

'Gordon, Nick Robinson, BBC News: why are you so shit?'

'John, why did you only embrace half of the bulimic experience?'

'Have you seriously never even had just one w*nk, Your Holiness?'

'Prince Harry, why have you got such thick red hair when all the other men in your family are balding?'

'Could you lend us a tenner, Mr Darling?'

'So Brooklyn, are you any relation to David and Victoria Beckham?'

'Boris, what are you doing?'

'Can I ask you to say all that again? My pen ran out.'

10. UNLIKELY PUB NAMES (Part 1)

THE HOSTILE ATMOSPHERE

THE ENTIRELY WHITE CLIENTELE

THE SLAPPER & HUSBAND

THE HOSTAGE'S HEAD

THE CHAPPED ARSE

THE STRANGE SMELL

THE GARY GLITTER

THE BOTTLED FACE

THE COCK & BLISTER

THE SOUTHERN POOF

THE KEG OF PISS

THE UNDERCOOKED CHICKEN

THE MISSILE & DUCK

THE UNSANITARY TOILETS

THE LEGIONNAIRES' OUTBREAK

THE STRAY DART

THE QUEEN'S IMPENDING DEATH

VLAD THE IMPALER

THE MAGGOT & SANDWICH

THE PAIR OF TITS

11. SURPRISING THINGS TO READ ON A LABEL (Part 1)

In the collar of a pair of Oxfam pyjamas: 'Unwashed since worn on deathbed'

School-Dinner Swizzlers – 'Ingredients: stuff, 99%; turkey, 1%'

Dog food – 'Ingredients: "Lucky Lad", fell at the first, Haydock'

Pot Noodle – 'Best after ten pints'

Ikea entertainment centre – 'Instructions not included, that should keep you entertained'

Duchy Original Hash cakes – 'Made to Prince Harry's own recipe'

'Pig scrotum – may contain nuts'

'Thai ladyboy – may contain nuts'

Burgers – 'Cooking instructions: flame grill on barbeque until carbon'

'Ready Meal for one ... sad lonely bastard'

Wet Suit – Dry Clean Only

12. REJECTED EXAM QUESTIONS
(Part 1)

1. Chemistry paper 2, question 1: using fertilizers and cleaning products, construct a bomb that can wipe out class 4B.

2. List your most sordid desires.

3. Tell me where the money is, all of it.

5. 'Bismarck was good for his country.' Ignore.

6. From memory, draw a picture of the Queen's bum.

7. If Pete has three ounces and Steve has seven, who will earn most at a nightclub?

8. Solve this equation using nothing more than the Internet...

9. 'David Miliband is a socialist icon.' Dismiss.

10. It takes two men ten minutes to check in for their flight – how long will it take Ahmed and Imran?

11. I wandered lonely as a what?

12. Do you suffer from erectile dysfunction?

13. If a budget flight leaves Stansted airport for its advertised destination of Stockholm but is actually due to land 100 miles away in neighbouring Denmark, how much money will you be refunded for the fact that the flight ends up being cancelled anyway?

14. Rearrange this sequence into the correct order: Sensibility and Sense.

15. What is courage? Putting 'this is' is not acceptable.

16. If you fail to get a grade A on this paper, what miniscule percentage of the population do you represent?

17. 'The use of computers makes students lazy.' Discuss, cutting and pasting your answer here.

18. What sells more copies of the *Daily Express*: house prices, or Diana's death?

19. Please describe your first sexual experience.

20. Describe how Newton's laws of motion affect the aerial flight of a sphere, if the seam down the middle has been picked at by a cheating foreign bowler.

21. English Literature GCSE, Question 1: Discuss the use of imagery and metaphor in *My Story So Far* by Wayne Rooney.

22. Thunderbirds are what?

13. UNLIKELY MEDICAL LABELS (Part 1)

Surgery hours 9.00am – 5.00pm

Warning:
If you're still
alive after five
minutes, you'll
be fine

Warning: tastes awful but that's the least of your troubles, pal, do you want boiled sweets or to stop the unbearable f*cking pain? Your choice.

May cause death.

Insert penis here.

Try operating heavy machinery for a laugh.

May cause funny jokes about the news if taken topically.

Crush up and smoke in pipe.

As not tested on anyone so far.

Rub on gums or ingest nasally, preferably from the buttocks of a call girl.

No rabbits were harmed during the testing of this product – but the rats were less lucky.

Insert anally ten times an hour.

Not quite ready yet.

Side-effects: may cause long uninterrupted erection if you're lucky.

Warning: did you see what happened to the six students we tested this on? No? Good.

May lead to bad language and scenes of a sexual nature from the outset.

May cause you to play the piano.

Do not take if planning to go out and get c***ed.

Insert three feet up rectum – you may need to borrow a friend's foot.

Do not take.

14. REJECTED FIRST LINES OF GREAT POEMS

In Xanadu did Kubla Khan / a branch of Tesco's once decree.

*Seasons of mists and mellow fruitfulness
Leaves on the line and sudden cancellations.*

*I wandered lonely through the crowd
Stealing credit cards and dollar bills.*

O my love is like a red, red cock, newly sprung at dawn.

*If you can keep your head when all about you are speaking
Arabic into a video camera…*

The Owl and the Pussycat went to sea, only one came back.

*Shall I compare thee to a summer's day?
Thou art as wet and disappointing, the trains are late, actually,
I say it's wet but with the bloody hosepipe ban…*

*Tyger, tyger burning bright
On my barbecue Tuesday night.*

*I met a traveller from an antique land who said,
'How I get British passport?'*

If I should die, think only this of me,
No one made me join the army.

They went to sea in a sieve, they did, in a sieve, the silly c**ts.

Half a league, half a league,
Between Man U and Liverpool these days.

O Wild West Wind, thou breath of Autumn's being,
Please blow up that woman's skirt.

In Xanadu did Mandelson / A useless f*cking Dome decree.

My heart aches and a drowsy numbness pains all down my
arms, f*ck I'm having a stroke!

How do I love thee? Let me count the ways…
Missionary, doggy and anal: three.

No man is an island, unless you count the Isle of Man.

Fifteen men on a dead man's chest,
Filming him on their phones.

It is the England goalkeeper / and he stoppeth one of three.

The Sea is calm tonight, but I'm shitting my pants.

'Twas the night before Christmas, when all through the house,
Burglars took everything, even my spouse.

15. IMPROBABLE TV LISTINGS

Saturday 14th

9.00 am Long Way Down
Finally, Ewan McGregor and Charley Boorman drive themselves and their f*cking motorbikes off the top of Canary Wharf.

9.30 am The Friday Night Project
Guest host Osama bin Laden joins Alan and Justin for knockabout fun and games.

11.00 am Escape to the Country
A convicted sex offender on the run is looking for a remote Scottish croft all but inaccessible from the mainland.

12.00 pm Loose Women
This week the panel take it in turns to fellate a screeching Dean Gaffney and a sweating Freddie Starr.

12.30 pm All-Star Family Fortunes
Former Nottingham Forest midfielder Ian Woan's family take on the man who used to play Winston in *Eastenders* and his relatives. Vernon Kay hosts.

1.00 pm Animal Park
Ben Fogle and Kate Humble shoot and skin tigers at Longleat. [repeat]

2.00 pm The Tudors
After emailing a greeting to the King of Spain, Henry helicopters himself to the 'Field of Cloth and Gold'.

3.00pm CELEBRITIES IN NEED
Terry Wogan is your reasonably priced host as a wealth of celebrities remind you of their talents and availability including: BBC Newsreaders pitching for light-entertainment work; the cast of Eastenders doing songs from the shows to help raise vital versatility on their showreels; a lazy version of an ailing panel-show format with celebrities too dull to do the actual show; and three hours of songs from the casts of West End shows with box office details on the screen throughout.

6.00 pm The 100 Greatest Things that Haven't Been in One of These Lists Already
Jimmy Carr presents.

6.30 pm Who Do You Think You Are?
Sir Patrick Moore explains that he is now convinced he is a fieldmouse in a story by Beatrix Potter.

7.30 pm FILM: Police Academy 34: Mission to Stockwell
Commissioner Blair lets the bungling cadets tackle a fleeing suspected suicide bomber at a London Underground station, with catastrophic consequences.

9.00 pm Heartbeat
A mysterious stranger arrives in

Aidensfield and either commits a crime or causes an accident. Featuring music that always makes you say, 'I didn't think this was from the Sixties.'

10.00 pm Time Team
Tony Robinson and the gang investigate some mysterious skeletons found in Rillington Place, London.

10.30 pm Bloodiest Ever You've Been Framed
Hilarious tea-time round-up of snuff movies, Jihadi calls to arms and underage pornography sent in by viewers.

11.00 pm Match of the Day
Thanks to satellite TV kick-offs, extended fifty-minute highlights of the only game of the day: Derby County versus Wigan Athletic. Messrs Lineker, Hansen and Shearer try to sound interested.

11.50 pm CSI Orkneys
Whilst investigating a child sex ring on a Sunday, Detective Brodie finds himself locked in a giant wicker effigy.

1.30 am An Audience with Nick Griffin
Near-the-knuckle humour from the BNP funny man, as an all-white celebrity audience joins in the japes.

2.00 am Countdown
98% of people who die do so during this programme.

2.30 am The X Factor
The results of next week's phone votes.

3.00 am Icons of the Seventies
Gary Glitter talks to Jonathan King... oh, someone really should have checked the tape before putting this out...

3.30 am Question Time
This week, David Dimbleby is pushing his own agenda in Winchester.

4.00 am 8 out of 10 Cats
Is this still on?

4.30 am Rick Stein's Mediterranean Escapes
The popular chef tunnels out of a Turkish prison with a homicidal drag queen.

5.00 am Chris Langham in the Psychiatrist's Chair
Episode 2 of 607.

6.00 am Who Do You Think You're Looking At?
Each week a celebrity goes into an East End pub, stares at people, spills pints and orders 'poofy drinks'.

CRITICS' CHOICE

★ **9.00 am The John Barrowman and Myleene Klass Show**
All the ubiquitous duo's TV appearances are consolidated into one easily manageable eight-hour daily chunk.

★ **11.00 am FILM: I Have A Moustache And I'm Shouting**
Historical epic starring Daniel Day Lewis.

★ **1.30 pm Derren Brown's Faustian Fun**
The sinister trickster buys the souls of tourists and students in Central London.

★ **2.00 pm Britain's Next Tabloid Target**
As the competition nears its climax, the girls try to impress judges Max Clifford, Kerry Katona and the editor of *OK!* magazine with their weight loss and drug intake.

★ **3.00 pm Ray Mears Goes Walkabout**
The posh adventurer explains how to survive a night in a branch of an Aussie-themed pub chain. This week: Wigan.

16. BAD THINGS TO HEAR ON WAKING UP

'You'll never find your penis where I threw it.'

'This is Radio 1 and you're listening to the Chris Moyles Breakfast Show...'

'Kippers?'

'Would you mind awfully taking my cock out of your mouth now?'

'Mummy ... I've made you a hamster sandwich for breakfast in bed!'

'Welcome to Broadmoor, Sexy.'

'Shit! He's coming round, pull his trousers up for me.'

'This is Big Brother, can one of the housemates please go to the diary room?'

'Earth to earth, ashes to ashes, dust to dust...'

'Now we do have something in common: chlamydia.'

'You've wet the bed again, Prime Minister.'

'Is this your car, sir?'

'What are you doing in the gorilla enclosure?'

'Dad, that was amazing.'

'We meet at last, Mr Bond.'

'Where has your house gone?'

'Hello, I'm Satan, we've been expecting you.'

'Eurrgh, who's that in your bed?'

'Oh leave him, he'll never get out of here alive now anyway.'

'Shit, he's waking up, nurse! Stop pissing about with his heart and I'll put it back in.'

'No, sorry, it wasn't a dream.'

'So, have I turned you gay then?'

'He's taken sixty now without bleeding.'

'Paul, we're taking you off and bringing on David James.'

'There is some bad news about your good kidney…'

'I'm Gillian McKeith and look what I've found in your sheets!'

17. DISCARDED ADVERTISING SLOGANS
(Part 1)

PLOP PLOP FIZZ FIZZ – THE SOUND FROM AMY WINEHOUSE'S TOILET

AND ALL BECAUSE THE LADY'S TAKEN OUT A RESTRAINING ORDER

BECAUSE YOU'RE WORTHLESS

SAY GOODBYE TO PERSISTENT FOOT PAIN WITH THIS CHAINSAW

MAYBE SHE'S BORN WITH IT, MAYBE IT'S A WIG?

THE MILK CHOCOLATE THAT MELTS IN YOUR POCKET, NOT IN YOUR HAND

MILKY WAY – THE SWEET YOU CAN EAT BETWEEN MEALS IF YOU REALLY
DON'T HAVE ANY WILLPOWER, YOU GREEDY BASTARD

GO TO WORK ON AN E

NO FT, NOT REALLY A PROBLEM

HAPPINESS IS A PIPE CALLED CRACK

FASTBUCK HOMES, BUILDING BOXES ON FLOOD PLAINS SINCE 1997

YOUR FRAGRANCE, YOUR FAULT

WHERE DO YOU WANT TO GO TODAY? WELL TOUGH, YOU'RE GOING TO BE
SAT AT YOUR DESK IN FRONT OF YOUR MICROSOFT COMPUTER AGAIN

YOU'LL WONDER WHERE THE YELLOW WENT WHEN YOU BRUSH WITH
ERASERDENT. COME TO THAT, YOU'LL WONDER WHERE YOUR
TEETH WENT

THE BEST A MAN CAN GET FOR A PALTRY AMOUNT

THE FUTURE'S BRIGHT IF YOU DON'T LIVE ON EARTH

COME TO SUNNY MARLBORO COUNTRY – WHICH MAY LEAD TO
LUNG CANCER

THE MAN FROM DEL MONTE, HE SAYS, 'I'M SURE I CAN BE PERSUADED
SOMEHOW, YOU BIG STRAPPING FARMER YOU'

WANNA DIE? JOIN THE PROFESSIONALS AND BE THE BEST

CARPET SALE ENDS MONDAY. NOT REALLY

NEW DIET DRINK WILL HELP YOU LOSE WEIGHT – YOU'LL GET CANCER
FROM ALL THE SWEETENER

CONSOLIDATE ALL YOUR DEBTS WITH US – AND YOUR HOUSE
WILL BE OURS IN A YEAR

18. UNLIKELY PUB NAMES (Part 2)

THE CAT & DYSENTERY

THE DONOR & LIVER

THE OMINOUS SILENCE

THE INBRED LOCALS

THE FAILING MARRIAGE

THE ROUGH & RACIST

THE COMPLEXION & ROSACEA

THE QUEEN'S CT**

THE BACK, SACK & CRACK

THE SNOT & BACON

THE CANNON & BALL

THE CHARLES KENNEDY

THE PARALYTIC & COMATOSE

THE SHOCK & AWE

THE BLOCKED TOILET

THE RING O' PAEDOPHILES

THE FOOT & MOUTH

THE SCRATCH & SNIFF

THE LEAKY SCROTUM

THE WITHERED ARMS

19. COMPUTER GAMES THAT WOULDN'T SELL (Part 1)

Sonic the Surveyor

Pro-Evolution Crown Green Bowls

Womb Raider

Super Miliband Brothers

Pokamom

Donkey Dong

Grand Theft Handbag

Parliamentary Motion

Dogger

Remains of the Day: The Game

Sex Crime 2: Tokyo

Luigi's Bungalow

Tony Hawk's Pro Fridge Carrier

Teach Yourself Walloon

Street Racing: Grifters

Fly Swatter 2

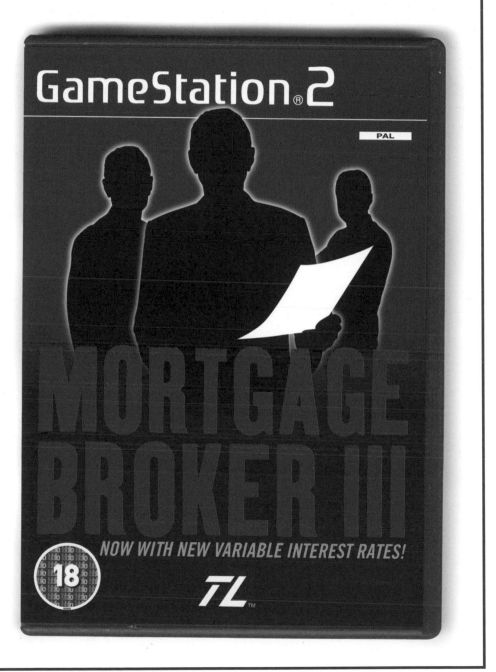

20. HYMNS THE CHURCH PREFERS TO FORGET

'Jesus H Christ'

'How Great Thou Arse'

'Christ on a Bike'

'It Was the Jews What Done It'

'Four and Twenty Virgins'

'Who's the Daddy?'

'While Shepherds Flashed their Cocks One Night'

'If You're Catholic and You Know It'

'Burn the Heretics, Hear the Scream'

'Don't Use a Johnny'

'In a Faraway Field, I was Shagged by the Priest'

'One John the Baptist, There's Only ...'

'That was Amazing, Grace!'

'I was Cold, I was Naked, Which I Know isn't an
Excuse but ...'

'Good King Wenceslas Came Out and Wed a Bloke
Called Stephen'

'Abide With Me, Lord, It Would Really Help
with the Mortgage'

'Once in Royal Tunbridge Wells'

'There's Holly and there's Ivy, You Should Hear
Them Groan'

21. UNLIKELY SMALL ADS (Part 2)

Phone for sale – call this number. If someone answers, it's already gone.

WANTED:
human guinea pig, for family pet.

FOR SALE:
4,996-piece jigsaw. No corners.

Call our sex line now – and ask a fat, ugly, middle-aged woman what colour knickers she's wearing.

Broken vase. One careful owner.

Original Rembrandt. £20 million, or nearest offer. Cash only for quick sale.

FOR SALE:
fully working torture rack, with spiked mask and iron ankle restraints. Unwanted gift.

Slightly rusty but much-loved needles – apply P. Doherty.

LOST:
marbles. If found, please return to T. Cruise, Hollywood.

FOR SALE:
rocket-powered car, three miles on clock, apply R. Hammond.

Trainee Swedish topless masseuse seeks flabby, middle-aged male to practise on. Will happily give sex in payment.

MADAME ZARA SEES THE FUTURE. YOU WILL NOT RING 020 6014 6056.

Taxi drivers needed; clean driving licence and knowledge of local area not required.

FOR SALE: one large tin, silver polish. Never used. Apply T. Henman.

Sperm clinic needs donors – please come quickly.

Want to make thousands of pounds fast? Tell me about it!

Baggage handlers required – £6 per hour, plus all the stuff you can nick.

ODD-JOB MAN: bricklaying, plastering and gynaecology.

Your name written on a grain of rice – no job too small.

Confused gay guy would like to meet similar. I enjoy naked fishing and being President of Russia.

Piping hot showers at any time of the day? Let me piss on you.

Complete collection of *Tomorrow's World* series. Only available on Betamax.

500 pairs of shoes, worn once or not at all. Apply any woman.

Tin of chewy toffee, no use to owner. Apply Shane MacGowan, the Arches, Waterloo Embankment.

FOR SALE: sat nav. Will deliver personally. Allow six months.

WANTED: metal dustbin lid. Must be sturdy. Apply Beagle 2, British Mars project.

22. LINES YOU WOULDN'T FIND IN A HARRY POTTER BOOK (Part 2)

'Overus Actus!' said Hermione.

And that, children, is why reading is bad for you.

That weird, thumping sound from the Forbidden Forest was the sound of a dead horse being flogged.

'Quick, if we use our broomsticks to fly to the top of the Tree of Enlightenment, we'll be able to see Hermione having a shower.'

'Do you realise we'll be thirty when they make the film of this one?' said Ron glumly.

The audience gasped as Harry got his cock out and blinded a horse.

'Mr Dumbledore, we'd like to question you about where you got some of these "magic" substances.'

'Oh no, Ron Weasley's hanged himself because he couldn't pay back his student loan.'

'Pass the tissues, Harry,' said Ron.

'Class, here's your new master of the dark arts, Mr Daniels.'

'Quick, Hermione, take this ageing potion – then we can fancy you legally.'

So after seven years, Harry left Hogwarts to hang in a glass box by Tower Bridge.

'This plot is rubbish,' said Harry. 'We need another special effect.'

Harry Potter had won – the evil witch JK Rowling would never write again.

So that's that, there is no God.

'There's nothing purer than the love between two men,' thought Ron as Harry eased out of him with a happy sigh.

'Is it meant to drip?' asked Ron.

'I am Voldemort, and I am gay!' said Voldemort. 'Let me show you some dark arts.'

In the first weeks of the new term, MRSA wiped out most of Griffyndor.

The Hogwarts Express had now been stuck in a siding outside Nuneaton for five hours.

It was a quiet term at Hogwarts. The End.

23. UNFORTUNATE NAMES FOR RACE HORSES (Part 1)

Distance: 2m 3f Prize money: £52,250 26 Runners and riders 2.30pm

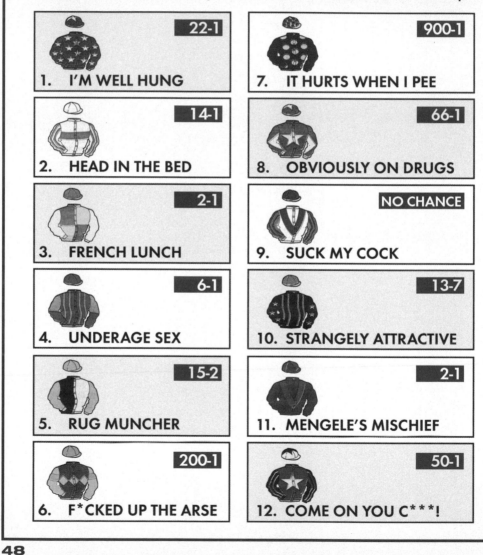

22-1 1. I'M WELL HUNG	**900-1** 7. IT HURTS WHEN I PEE
14-1 2. HEAD IN THE BED	**66-1** 8. OBVIOUSLY ON DRUGS
2-1 3. FRENCH LUNCH	**NO CHANCE** 9. SUCK MY COCK
6-1 4. UNDERAGE SEX	**13-7** 10. STRANGELY ATTRACTIVE
15-2 5. RUG MUNCHER	**2-1** 11. MENGELE'S MISCHIEF
200-1 6. F*CKED UP THE ARSE	**50-1** 12. COME ON YOU C***!

20-1
13. I'M LEAVING YOU, YOU BITCH

5-1
14. UNSIGHTLY RASH

3-1
16. RUSSIAN ANUS

1000-1
17. JAILBAIT

250-1
18. PRITT STICK

10-1
19. SHITS WHERE IT LIKES

8-1
20. SMOTHERED THE TWINS

18-1
21. ELECTRODES TO THE GONADS

33-1
22. PHILIP'S A RACIST

UTTER DONKEY
23. JANETTE KRANKIE'S MINGE

6-1
24. STICKY DISCHARGE

15-2
25. PETER SUTCLIFFE'S DELIGHT

7-1
26. CAT MEAT

24. ILL-ADVISED FIRST LINES OF BIOGRAPHIES

'Nothing interesting ever happens to me.'

'My name is Ann Widdecombe and I'm going to talk to you about my sex life.'

'It's not easy being Alan Titchmarsh's brother.'

'I've got a pain in my arm, I don't feel welllllllllll lllllllllllllllll...'

'Andreas Pankarisos is my real name, but you know me as Andy Pandy.'

'But that's enough about me.'

'Let's begin at the beginning: first a swirling cloud of cosmic gas cooled to form what we call the Sun...'

'You will like this autobiography, but not a lot.'

'I hope you won't find my life as boring as I have.'

'This is all about my lifelong struggle with amnesia.'

'Speaking as a mayfly...'

'Now, child-killers don't always get a good press...'

'I vividly recall the time
It first occurred to me to rhyme...'

'I was named Cliff Richard but not THE Cliff Richard.'

'People always ask me how I first came up with the idea for the paper-clip.'

'I always were and always would be a terrible writerer.'

'Colonic irrigation has always fascinated me, as this 'scratch 'n' sniff' autobiography illustrates.'

'Calm down dear, it's only my autobiography.'

'I was inspired to write by Salman Rushdie's brilliant *Satanic Verses*.'

'I suppose most people know me as Private Sponge from *Dad's Army*, but this is the story of the real Colin Bean.'

'It's always been tough being a narcoleptic and zzzzzz zzzzzzzzzzzzzzzz.'

'They call me the World's Most Irritating Man. How unfair. Hear ye, history will judge me differently after this... read on, McDuff! (I know it should be "Lead on" but this is a joke and don't worry, it isn't the last...)'

'The first thing I should tell you is that I'm not really blind and Sadie is just a pet.'

'OK, so my sisters moved to England, had a hit and one dated a politician, but what about the brother they left behind in Romania – the Cheeky Boy?'

25. PET FOOD ADS THAT WOULD BE BANNED

KWIK-SICK — JUST ADD WATER FOR THE
PERFECT MEAL FOR YOUR PET PIGEON

NEW MONSIEUR DOG WITH FROG AND
HORSE CHUNKS IN A GARLIC SAUCE

NEW LICKABLE, MEATY BODY PAINT —
HOURS OF FUN FOR YOU AND YOUR DOG

9 OUT OF 10 OWNERS SAID THEIR CATS
ACTUALLY PREFERRED EATING THEIR OWN SHIT

LOYD GROSSMAN'S RABBIT AND BLACKBIRD
IN A POMODORO SAUCE

THE NEW ROTTWEILER MEALS RANGE
COMES IN TODDLER, POSTMAN AND
VULNERABLE OAP FLAVOUR

NEW PAL WITH BONE MARROW

NEW BLUE TONGUE —THE TASTE YOUR
SHEEP WILL DIE FOR

INSTANT DOG MEAL — JUST ADD URINE

MR SNIFFER DOG: NOW IN CORPSE, HEROIN
AND SEMTEX FLAVOURS

26. UNLIKELY FRONT-PAGE HEADLINES

AT LAST! ANN WIDDECOMBE TOPLESS

COMPLICATED STOCK EXCHANGE FRAUD – FULL DETAILS INSIDE

MY INCREDIBLE 45 MINUTES EACH WAY WITH
SUPER STUD PHIL NEVILLE

GEORGE MICHAEL IS GAY – FAKE SHEIKH EXPOSÉ

LOTS OF ANTS FOUND IN THE WORLD

JFK DEAD – OFFICIAL

FREDDIE STARR ATE MY HAM

FREE INSIDE: 'WOMEN OF THE CABINET' CHARITY CALENDAR

GOTCHA! MAN CAUGHT SPEEDING ON MOTORWAY

PHEW! HOTTEST DAY SINCE 2007

SOME TRAINS DELAYED ... A BIT

DIANA ENQUIRY LATEST

DYSLEXIC TYPESETTER GIVEN THE SOCK

F*CK! WAR!

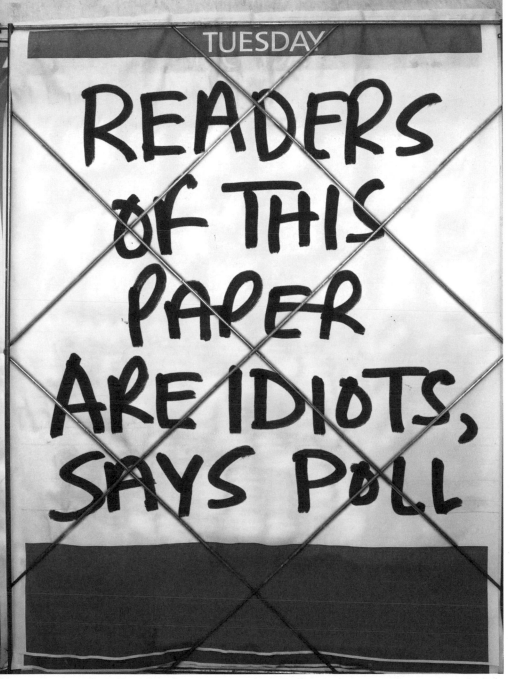

27. FAMOUS LAST WORDS YOU DIDN'T HEAR

'I SAY, DODI, ISN'T THAT CAMILLA AND CHARLES IN THAT WHITE FIAT UNO?'

'THANKS, I'M VERY PROUD OF "IMAGINE"... IS THAT MARK WITH A "C", MR CHAPMAN?'

'CHARLES, WHAT ARE YOU DOING IN HERE WITH THAT PILLOW?'

'YOU MIGHT BE WONDERING WHY THEY'RE CALLED A STINGRAY. CRIKEY!'

'WE ARE SADDAM'S SONS, THE AMERICANS WOULD NOT DARE.'

'TELL TONY HIS TRUSTY DEPUTY IS HAVING ONE OF THEM CARDIGAN, CADILLAC, A CARILOKIE ARREST ... OH BUGGER, I'VE DROPPED ME CHIPS...'

'IT'S NOT LOADED, LOOK.'

'PRIME MINISTER, WOULD YOU SIGN MY RUCKSACK?'

'I'M TOUCHED – I'VE NEVER SEEN SO MANY RABBIS AT ONE OF MY PREMIERES BEFORE, SUGARTITS.'

'THEY WOULDN'T DARE SHOOT AN ARCHDUKE, THINK OF THE TROUBLE THAT WOULD CAUSE.'

'I INVENTED THE ATKINS DIET, ANOTHER DOUGHNUT'S NOT GOING TO KILL ME.'

'I'M TELLING YOU, THAT REGGIE KRAY'S A BIG FAT POOF.'

'IT'S ONLY ONE TILE, IT CAN'T DO THAT MUCH DAMAGE TO THE SHUTTLE.'

'I GOT IT OFF EBAY, BUT IT'S THE BEST MINE DETECTOR IN THE MARKE–'

'NOTHING, MEIN FÜHRER, IT'S JUST A COUPLE OF ASPIRINS.'

'I HOPE YOU BLOODY KNIGHTS HAVE WIPED YOUR FEET BEFORE BLUNDERING YOUR WAY INTO MY CATHEDRAL.'

'AT LAST, I, KING CHARLES III, ON THE DAY OF MY CORONATION...'

'MUGABE? NO, I VOTED FOR TSVANGIRAI.'

'CAN YOU POP BACK LATER, O.J.? I'VE GOT A FRIEND ROUND.'

'FREE TIBET!'

'I'M AFRAID YOU'VE HAD A WASTED TRIP, DR SHIPMAN, I FEEL FINE NOW.'

'LOOK, HENRY: WE'VE HAD A BEAUTIFUL BABY GIRL! LET'S CALL HER MARY TUDOR.'

28. UNLIKELY EMAILS TO FIND IN YOUR INBOX

Outbox
Sent Items
Deleted Items
Junk E-mail
Microsoft News Server
Microsoft News Server 1
▶ Mail Views

We are doing a survey to see how alike people's bank details are. Please send us yours. We are honest. Honest.

I'm a Nigerian general – just wondering how things are with you?

Hi, I'm a really sexy and cool woman of your dreams and I spend all my time logged in to Internet dating sites as well.

You have actually won an hourly prize, here it is.

This is your Internet banking service. We have put too much money in your account this month, so you may as well keep it.

Is your erection functioning perfectly?

Hello, son, it's your mum here, I've just uploaded some JPEGs onto your zipdrive, I'll try and import some Firefox cookies over to your hard drive a bit later on...

Mail

Address Book

Calendar

Notes

Tasks

Project Center

Hide Folders

Folders on My Computer
- Inbox
- Drafts
- Outbox
- Sent Items
- Deleted Items
- Junk E-mail

Microsoft News Server

Microsoft News Server 1

Mail Views

Inbox

From | contains | Search

From | Subject

▼ Today

Hello, my name is Pete Townshend, I'd like to browse a porn site for research for a book I'm writing, but thought I should notify the relevant authorities first.

Bless me, Father, for I have sinned; it is six months since my last confession...

I know we haven't spoken for ages but it's fine, I don't want anything, just thought I'd say hello.

No milk today, please.

REPLY ALL: Will you marry me? Yes/no/can I get back to you [delete as appropriate].

How would you like a penis reduction?

Titslutjizzbucket16 would like to offer you a new low-interest credit card.

Hi. I don't know how to use email.

Xvtruc%987234.99.xcernm.99v says 'Hi Mate. How are you? Long time no see.'

Hey Big Boy, it's Katy. Are we still having our torrid affair on Wednesdays when my husband Ian is at football training? Just let me know. Love, Katy. (Not Ian, definitely not.)

29. UNLIKELY CROSSWORD CLUES (Part 1)

8 **9**

16 **17** **18**

19

20 **21**

22

ACROSS

1 Hooray for the Gunners – sorry love, I changed lanes by accident – the ascent of Gary Glitter (2, 3, 4)

8 Things that my dick has been said to be (4)

9 Rip van Winkle's name (3, 3, 6)

10 Wife berates recalcitrant husband 'You f_____ c____!' (7, 4)

11 Columnist on this newspaper that no one likes (6, 8)

14 My wife's nickname for my penis (7)

15 Something that will get you a fatwa (6, 8, 7)

16 Are you a paedo? (3)

17 Guess my name or I can have your first-born daughter (15)

20 Irritating f*cking Japanese numbers game that everyone prefers to crosswords now (2, 4)

21 Your innermost secret (fill in the whole grid and send in)

22 BlahblahohwhatsthepointIvebeendoingthistoolong

30. UNAPPETISING THINGS TO READ ON A MENU (Part 2)

Vegetarian option: something horrible with tofu

Tin de Hoops de Spaghetti

Poulet à la Flu

Potato stuffed inside a pig's arse

No exchanging, no sharing, no kindness of any sort

Today's Special: Whole Cow (select your own)

Whole sea bass at market price (but it's a seriously expensive market)

Today's set menus:

1. 'Wow! That's Pricey'
2. 'You Have to Be Kidding'
*3. 'F*ck me!'*

* Indicates low fat ** Indicates low fat and tasteless

Japanese breakfast: some bitter things and some stuff with the consistency of snot

Select your own fish and then butcher it, you heartless bastard

31. THINGS YOU NEVER HEAR ON THE RADIO

'You're listening to 6-0-6, two hours of whining about referees…'

'My telly career never took off because I'm plug ugly.'

'And as you can hear, the black ball is right against the cushion, behind three reds.'

'This is Capital Radio and that's enough adverts – now, back to the adverts.'

'Attention all shipping – buy a radar, this isn't the 1930s.'

'Now Clement Freud, let's have "just a minute" on the joy of fisting.'

'For those of you at home, the Archbishop of Canterbury is wearing a gimp mask.'

'And now here's that ugly bird with the travel.'

'And now, another patronising edition of *Woman's Hour*.'

'Good evening and welcome to the Bridlington Mime Festival…'

'This is Radio 3, and if you're both listening I'll put on that Beethoven CD.'

'And as you join us here at Lord's, the batsman's holding the bowler's wil– oh sod it, they're just having gay sex.'

'Here's some travel advice: if you want to get anywhere, buy a helicopter.'

'Hi, you're listening to Mike Reid – the one that didn't die.'

'And now *The Archers*, and Old Seth has just been caught cottaging in Ambridge High Street…'

'So it's 4 a.m. listeners, and I'm the only thing between you and suicide.'

'And new in at number one, having sold sixteen copies, it's…'

'Before we close on Radio 4, it's time for "A W*nk at Bedtime".'

'And you've gone for an unusual desert island luxury … six hookers and a wrap of crack.'

32. QUESTIONS OMITTED FROM THE BRITISH CITIZENSHIP TEST (Part 1)

1. In a transport cafeteria, does one stub out a cigarette into the yolk or the white of an egg?

2. If someone barges ahead of you in a queue, is the correct response 'ch' or 'tt'?

3. Who has contributed most to the musical landscape of Britain: Edward Elgar, Benjamin Brittain, or Howard from the Halifax?

4. Name one Channel Four programme apart from *Big Brother*.

5. Which side of the road should you drive on when chased by the police?

6. What volume should you set your ringtone to on the train, to ensure that everyone can hear it?

7. Just what does it say on a tin of Ronseal?

8. What is the correct etiquette for vomiting in a taxi? Kerbside window, offside window or straight on the floor?

9. What does Kerry Katona do?

10. Can you believe it's not butter?

11. Which phrase do we most popularly associate with Churchill? 'We will fight them on the beaches' or 'Oh yus'?

12. What is the correct way to see off a Jehovah's Witness?

13. Have you ever taken part in genocide? If so, what was it like?

14. How did you travel to this country? a) By plane b) Walking through the channel tunnel or c) Hiding in the back of a lorry full of tomatoes?

15. Name three insults you should shout when Frank Lampard has the ball in a football match.

16. Can you read English? If not, please go to question 20.

17. Complete the following phrase: 'Pugh, Pugh, Barney McGrew…'

18. For Eastern European nationals only. Please tick which of the following best describes you: a) a plumber b) a lap dancer c) a credit-card cloner or d) all of the above.

19. Are you good enough to represent this country in the 2012 Olympics? If not, can you play tennis?

20. Can you still not read bloody English?

21. Estimate to the nearest decade the age of Bruce Forsyth.

33. UNLIKELY T-SHIRT SLOGANS

AMY
WINEHOUSE
EUROPEAN TOUR 2008

CA **CANCELLED** 14

MAN **CANCELLED** NE 17

GLA **CANCELLED** E 19

EDIN **CANCELLED** E 20

LOND **CANCELLED** /24/25

P **CANCELLED** 8

MA **CANCELLED** LY 1

M **CANCELLED** 3

N **CANCELLED** 7

I'M AN ANNOYING TEENAGER WHO THINKS T-SHIRT
SLOGANS ARE FUNNY

I ♥ TRANSPLANT

IF YOU CAN READ THIS YOU'RE DANCING TOO CLOSE

MY BOYFRIEND WENT TO IBIZA AND ALL HE BROUGHT ME BACK WAS
THIS LOUSY SYPHILIS

CERTIFIED SEX INSTRUCTOR
(THOUGH OBVIOUSLY I'M STILL A VIRGIN)

Front: 'HEAD GOES HERE, RIGHT ARM HERE, LEFT ARM HERE'
Back: W. ROONEY, 9

IF YOU CAN READ THIS YOU PROBABLY WEREN'T STATE EDUCATED

THIS ISN'T A T-SHIRT JUST A REALLY BRUTAL WEDGIE

ALL POLICEMEN ARE RACISTS

MAX MOSLEY SMACKED MY ARSE

I'M SUPPORTING ENGLAND IN EURO 2008

PUNCH ME IF YOU THINK YOU'RE HARD ENOUGH

GIULIANI FOR PRESIDENT!

HERE, LOOK AT MY TITS

THIS ISN'T RED, I'VE JUST BEEN STABBED BY A HOODIE

34. LIES FROM EVERYDAY LIFE (Part 1)

'THERE IS A GOOD SERVICE ON ALL LONDON UNDERGROUND LINES.'

'NO, IT WASN'T ME, IT MUST HAVE BEEN THE DOG.'

'YES, YOUR PENIS IS BIGGER THAN MY PREVIOUS BOYFRIEND'S.'

'YOU'LL GET IT TOMORROW, I SENT IT FIRST CLASS.'

'YOUR CALL IS VERY IMPORTANT TO US.'

'THIS SUMMER'S MUST HAVE.'

'YOU'VE HAD A FACELIFT? I NEVER WOULD HAVE KNOWN.'

'YOU'D NEVER KNOW IT WAS QUORN.'

'OF COURSE IT DOESN'T PUT ME OFF, HEATHER.'

'I'M NOT A RACIST BUT...'

'A WATCHED POT NEVER BOILS.'

'I BOUGHT THIS WRISTBAND BECAUSE I PASSIONATELY BELIEVE IN ERADICATING POVERTY.'

'NO THANKS, I'VE ALREADY BOUGHT A BIG ISSUE THIS WEEK.'

'IT'S MY GLANDS.'

'YOUR MINICAB WILL BE WITH YOU IN TWO MINUTES.'

'IT'S NOT YOU, IT'S ME.'

'OH WAS SHE NOT WEARING A BRA? I DIDN'T NOTICE.'

'I'VE NO IDEA HOW THAT SITE GOT ONTO MY INTERNET "HISTORY". MUST BE A VIRUS.'

'SORRY DARLING, IT SLIPPED UP THERE BY ACCIDENT.'

'NO DARLING, THAT FITS BEAUTIFULLY.'

'NO, I DIDN'T VOTE FOR BORIS.'

'THE WINNER OF THE PEOPLE'S CHOICE COMEDY AWARD IS ... ANT AND DEC!'

'THE MANAGER HAS OUR FULL SUPPORT.'

'I HAVE NO COMMENT ON THE KISS AND TELL, IT IS IN THE HANDS OF MY LAWYERS.'

35. GREETINGS CARDS THAT WOULDN'T SELL (Part 2)

Sorry to hear the condom split

Happy new breasts!

From an aunt who doesn't know you very well

Wishing you a very happy fatwa

Congratulations on your first ejaculation

Kim Jong, Sorry to hear you're Il

To a special 'Uncle'

Congratulations on your one-month wedding anniversary – we all gave it two weeks

Sorry to hear you're now on the sex offenders' register

Thank you for swallowing

Now you are One (contains message inside: Congratulations on coming out!)

Congratulations on your regime change (also available: So sorry to hear you've been toppled)

At last you've passed a solid!

36. PUBLIC TRANSPORT ANNOUNCEMENTS YOU'LL NEVER HEAR

'As we pull out of Bristol Temple Meads, I'd like to read to you from my as yet unpublished novel.'

'As the weather is so hot, we will switch on the air conditioning.'

'These tickets are real value for money.'

'And just behind the buffet car is the jacuzzi.'

'I never feel safer than when I'm in an empty carriage in the middle of the night, near Reading.'

'We're getting there, but really slowly.'

'If you look out the window, you will see the same thing you saw two hours ago.'

'I wonder what the age of this train really is?'

'For those of you unable to read screens, boards, the front of trains or believe any of the passengers around you, the train you have just seemingly taken a punt on boarding is going to Southampton.'

'Choose from one of 107 different fares.'

'The bar is now open for sandwiches, chocolate and scalding-hot water.'

'Get your dicks ou ... tickets, I meant tickets.'

'You're on the Penzance to Inverness, and this is James Blunt...'

'If you look down the toilets, you can see the track!'

'That little bobbly thing that you put your foot on to work the flush ... will not work.'

'There'll be a selection of crisps and cold and tepid drinks.'

'After I say "go", the first person to pull the emergency cord wins £10.'

'You will need to take a rail replacement coach all the way, so we will happily charge you less for the journey.'

'If you're an attractive young woman, you may want to make your way to Carriage C, where a highly respected judge will be exposing his penis.'

'Coach E is for any single people who might like to size up the talent.'

'Owing to a fatality at Clapham Junction, this train is currently driverless and heading into the buffers at East Croydon at 167 m.p.h.'

'If you're interested in seeing some history during your journey, can I draw your attention to the toilets in Coach F; they haven't been flushed since 1988 and contain some of the finest fossilized stools in the country.'

37. REJECTED SLOGANS FOR THE LONDON OLYMPICS

LONDON 2012
WAY OVER
BUDGET

SOME MISTAKE SURELY?

WE'RE NOT FAR FROM PARIS

LET'S HOPE WE DON'T GET BOMBED

A SILVER ON THE LAST DAY

SORRY ABOUT THE TRANSPORT

COULD BE WORSE, YOU COULD BE IN MANCHESTER

WHO CARES?

COME FOR THE OLYMPICS, STAY FOR ASYLUM

LARGELY STEROID FREE

AT LEAST WE'LL WIN THE ROWING

EAT OUR SHORTS PARIS

WE'RE TAKING THE URINE

LONDON 2013 – BETTER LATE THAN NEVER

HIGHER, FURTHER, FASTER, MORE EXPENSIVE

IS THAT A STARTING PISTOL IN YOUR POCKET,
OR ARE YOU MUGGING ME?

HACKNEY MARSHES – A SOLID FOUNDATION FOR
THE OLYMPICS

UK GOLD – STILL JUST A TV CHANNEL

38. LINES YOU WON'T FIND IN THE BIBLE (Part 1)

SO JESUS MADE THEM ALL BACON SANDWICHES.

'I HAVEN'T GOT ANY SWADDLING I'M AFRAID,' SAID THE INNKEEPER, 'BUT THERE IS THIS OLD ROMPER SUIT.'

'SORRY, THE MYRRH GOT CONFISCATED BY CUSTOMS.'

'YOU'RE BANG OUT OF ORDER PHARAOH, DO YOU KNOW WHAT I MEAN?' SAID MOSES.

AND ON THE EIGHTH DAY HE DIDN'T DO MUCH BECAUSE IT WAS A BANK HOLIDAY.

'DO THAT AGAIN EVE,' SAID ADAM, 'BUT FIRST LICK YOUR LIPS... YEAH?'

JONAH WAS SWALLOWED BY A GIANT FISH AND DECIDED THAT NOW WAS THE TIME TO LAY OFF LSD.

'I TOLD YOU WE SHOULD MAKE A RESERVATION,' SHOUTED MARY, 'IT'S BLOODY CHRISTMAS.'

'FOLLOW THE STAR? TONIGHT? IT'S THE FINAL OF *X FACTOR*.'

'SHIT! THERE'S A F*CKING LION IN HERE!' SAID DANIEL.

'How shall I build the Ark, Lord?' asked Noah. 'With this allen key,' said God.

'I'm telling Mum,' said Isaac.

'Best of three?' said Goliath's big brother as David wheeled away in triumph.

'There's three of us in this marriage,' said Joseph.

And lo, all the creatures of land and sea evolved gradually over millions of years.

And Abraham did beget Isaac and Isaac did beget Jacob, and Jacob was gay so that was the end of that.

Though shalt take thy healing crystals, sit under a pyramid and chant 'Ommm'.

In the beginning was the word and the word was... 'contifabulation'. Sandy Toksvig goes first!

'Good news, Jesus,' said Pontius Pilate, 'I'm commuting your sentence to "life".'

Slowly, tenderly, Joseph's fingers inched up Mary's silken thigh.

And so the Messiah was born, on a day that would for ever be celebrated as ... Winterval.

39. COMPETITIONS NO-ONE WOULD ENTER

★ GET HUMPED BY A DOBERMAN-A-THON ★

★ WIN A FARM IN ZIMBABWE ★

★ GMTV'S LATEST PHONE VOTE ★

★ HOW MUCH ASBESTOS CAN YOU INHALE? ★

★ WIN A CHANCE TO JOIN THE DOTS ON
DEAN GAFFNEY'S FACE ★

★ WHO'S GOT BRITAIN'S TINIEST COCK? ★

★ WIN A TREKKING HOLIDAY WITH JIMMY SAVILE ★

★ THE BAGHDAD MARATHON ★

★ JOIN SAGA TODAY AND ENTER A DRAW TO SHAG
WAYNE ROONEY ★

★ STICK YOUR HAND IN THIS HOLE ★

★ AL-QAEDA 'PASS THE PARCEL' ★

★ WIN CHERIE BLAIR'S GREATEST HITS ★

★ THREE LUCKY MIRROR READERS CAN BE CIRCUMCISED
TOMORROW ★

★ AN ALL-EXPENSES-PAID TRIP TO KFC ★

★ **STRICTLY CUM** ★

★ **SPOT THE BALL AND WIN A CHANCE TO SERVE IN AFGHANISTAN FOR TWO WEEKS** ★

★ **YOUR CHANCE TO TAKE PART IN CHEMICAL TRIALS FOR A NEW DRUG** ★

★ **MISS IRAN** ★

★ **A DRINKING CONTEST WITH CHARLES KENNEDY** ★

★ **ELEPHANT MAN LOOKALIKE COMPETITION** ★

★ **READER'S DIGEST PRIZE DRAW** ★

★ **WIN A THONG WORN BY PETER STRINGFELLOW** ★

★ **CLEANEST FRENCHMAN** ★

★ **BRITAIN'S MEANEST MAN – ENTRY £1** ★

★ **WIN A TEN-MINUTE TROLLEY DASH AT LIDL** ★

★ **WIN A TWO-WEEK HOLIDAY FOR FIVE IN DONCASTER** ★

★ **MEET THE STARS OF HIGH SCHOOL MUSICAL (WELL, THE ONES WHO ARE OVER 30)** ★

★ **SIGN UP FOR THE NATIONAL DNA DATABASE AND WIN AN ELECTRONIC ANKLE BRACELET** ★

★ **WIN TICKETS FOR A BEN ELTON MUSICAL** ★

★ **ROUND AUSTRALIA SWIMMING RACE** ★

★ **MR GAY ALABAMA** ★

★ **WIN A LUNCH DATE WITH VANESSA FELTZ** ★

40. DISCARDED HEADLINES FROM HISTORY

DIANA MARRIES CHARLES IN PARTNERSHIP DOOMED TO END IN NASTY CAR ACCIDENT IN PARIS

AS JESUS DIES, WE ASK 'WHERE'S YOUR TEARS, MARY?'

ANOTHER RIPPER VICTIM! TO ADD TO YOUR WALLCHART STICKER COLLECTION

ASTEROID STRIKE: MANY DINOSAURS DEAD

FIRST EVER TRAIN JOURNEY (20 MINUTES LATE, SIGNAL FAILURE AT CLAPHAM JUNCTION)

CATHERINE OF ARAGON: 'THERE ARE THREE OF US IN THIS MARRIAGE'

FROGS, LOCUSTS, DARKNESS – IS CLIMATE CHANGE RUINING EGYPT?

'FIRE WAS MY IDEA' CLAIM INVENTOR'S FRIENDS

'NOT IN OUR NAME' HUNS TAKE TO STREETS TO PROTEST ATTILA'S INVASION OF GAUL

BUBONIC PLAGUE – AMERICAN LAB LIKELY SOURCE?

HENRY VIII – READ ABOUT MY BIRDS, THE BOOZE AND THE BLOODBATHS, ONLY IN THIS SUNDAY'S NEWS OF THE WORLD

BRITAIN DECLARES WAR ON GERMANY, HOW WILL IT EFFECT HOUSE PRICES?

2966 WORLD CUP SPECIAL – CAN ENGLAND END 1,000 YEARS OF HURT?

RAMESES CRITICISED OVER WEIRD POINTY TOMB THING

41. LIES FROM EVERYDAY LIFE (Part 2)

'SORRY, MATE, I HAVEN'T GOT ANY SPARE CHANGE.'

'THANK YOU, GRANNY, THAT WAS DELICIOUS.'

'SOCKS – JUST WHAT I WANTED!'

'I'D LOVE TO COME BUT WE'RE AWAY THAT WEEKEND.'

'NO, I REALLY CAN'T SPARE TWO MINUTES FOR YOUR CHARITY.'

'I JUST HAD THE ONE QUICK DRINK AFTER WORK, BUT THE TRAFFIC HOME WAS TERRIBLE.'

'YOU'LL REALLY GO PLACES WITH THIS MEDIA STUDIES DEGREE.'

'REMEMBER, YOUR VOTE COUNTS.'

'THERE'S A CALLER AT THE FRONT DOOR – I HOPE IT'S THAT MAN SELLING OVERPRICED J-CLOTHS.'

'100% BEEF'.

'I'D HAPPILY STOP FLYING TO PREVENT GLOBAL WARMING.'

'YOU'VE GOT TO ADMIRE RICHARD BRANSON.'

'I LOVE YOU, LEMBIT.'

'THE EDEN PROJECT – WHAT A GREAT DAY OUT.'

'WE NEED A RANGE ROVER IN SURBITON.'

'IT'S NOT EXAMS THAT HAVE GOT EASIER; CHILDREN ARE JUST CLEVERER THESE DAYS.'

'THAT VICTORIA BECKHAM, SHE'S A LOOKER ISN'T SHE?'

'THE AMERICANS HAVE THE SITUATION IN IRAQ UNDER CONTROL.'

'THAT NAZI COSTUME WILL GO DOWN A TREAT, HARRY.'

'I DID NOT SEE THE PENALTY INCIDENT.'

'YOUR SAFETY IS OUR PRIORITY.'

'I'VE NO IDEA WHERE OUR SHANNON IS.'

'THE ONLY REASON WE HAVE TO FINISH IS BECAUSE I LOVE YOU TOO MUCH.'

'TO HAVE AND TO HOLD, FOR BETTER OR WORSE, FOR RICHER OR POORER...'

42. UNLIKELY FIRST LINES FOR LOVE SONGS

"You remind me of the M1."

"I love you too much to let you live."

"I don't mean any of this, I'm just angling for a shag."

"I would shave my armpits for you."

"You're the (next) best thing."

"You took out your dentures."

"It started with a fist..."

"Run your fingers through my back hair."

"Tie me up and put an orange in my mouth."

"Get your tits out for the lads."

"You kept me in your basement until I was eighteen."

"I've still got the herpes to remember you by."

"Our death pact is strong."

"I love you like the E4791 steam train from Newcastle."

"I'll love you for the rest of your life ... when the farmer takes you off to slaughter."

"We met on the net and I ate you."

43. TERRIBLE NAMES FOR CARS

The 4X4 Haemorrhage

The Peugeot Perineum

The Vauxhall Hawking

The Citroën Closet Homosexual

The Hyundai Affordable

The Peugeot Garlic

The Honda Scrotum

The Ford Badger

The Hatchback Deathtrap

The Robin Repugnant

The Nissan Tank Top

The Toyota Su-Doku

The Fiat Embarrassino

The Mitsubishi Dogger

The Volkswagen Risible

The Nissan Cumbersome

The Ford Schmord

The Reliant Rubber

The Renault Smoker

The Mitsubishi Smegma

The Volvo Sven

The Renault Asylum

The Volkswagen Führer

The Fiat Pederast

The Citroën Fiasco

The Lamborghini Mussolini

The BMW Smug

The Penis Substitute

The Honda Mediocre

The Renault Shipman

The Vauxhall Vulva

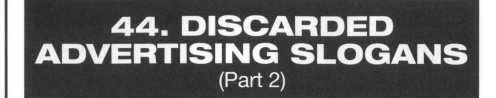

44. DISCARDED ADVERTISING SLOGANS
(Part 2)

CURRY SAUCE-FLAVOURED CONDOMS – FOR WHEN YOU PULL A BIFFA

BP – IT MIGHT LOOK LIKE A FLOWER, BUT IT'S STILL F*CKING PETROL

TO BE HONEST, ONE RAZOR BLADE IS QUITE ENOUGH

WE AT SAINSBURY'S SAY 'TRY SOMETHING NEW TODAY'.
LIKE SHOPPING AT TESCO!

THERE ARE A LOT OF SEXY GIRLS IN THIS ADVERT, BUT TO BE HONEST,
ALL LAGER TASTES THE SAME

SWITCH YOUR MORTGAGE TO US – THE BANK THAT LIKES TO
REPOSSESS

CADBURY'S FLAKE – YOU'RE MEANT TO THINK IT'S A COCK

HOW HAIRY ARE YOUR TESTICLES?

DESPITE THE LILTING IRISH VOICEOVER, NEVER FORGET: IT'S ONLY CIDER

WAP-BASED PROTOCOL, INTERNET APPLICATIONS AND BLUETOOTH
CONNECTIVITY ... ARE JUST THREE THINGS YOU'LL NEVER USE ON THIS
OVERPRICED PHONE

NEW TAMPONS – RUN, SWIM, EAT CHOCOLATE, BITE YOUR HUSBAND'S HEAD OFF

CONDOMS – RIBBED INSIDE AND OUT. WHY SHOULD SHE HAVE ALL THE FUN?

TASTY CRISPS NOW IN NEW MESQUITE CHICKEN AND THYME FLAVOUR – WELL, IT'S A BUNCH OF CHEMICALS AND E NUMBERS REALLY

THIS IS A CLASSY AND VERY FUNNY AD – BUT YOU'LL NEVER REMEMBER WHAT IT'S FOR

THIS IS OUR LOGO – TO BE HONEST, WE'RE AS DISAPPOINTED AS YOU ARE

POISON – IT DOES EXACTLY WHAT IT SAYS ON THE TIN

WE SAY OUR PASTA SAUCE IS MADE IN THE EU TO CONJURE UP IMAGES OF SUN BAKED ITALIAN FIELDS, RATHER THAN THE GREY INDUSTRIAL SHEDS IN HOLLAND WHERE IT'S ACTUALLY MADE

BRITISH AIRWAYS, THE WORLD'S FAVOURITE AIRLINE. IF THE COMPANY'S PAYING

TAKE TWO BOTTLES INTO THE SHOWER? YOU'VE GOT TWO HANDS, WHY NOT?

YOU CAN BUY THIS CAR IF YOU LIKE, BUT YOU'LL NEVER GO THIS FAST YOURSELF

45. UNLIKELY SMALL ADS (Part 3)

WOULD LIKE TO MEET:
Female. Age – any. Looks – any. Requirements: two tits and a heartbeat. Apply R. Brand.

I'm a 14-year-old girl looking for a 45–55 man for online webcam fun. Email me : operationlolita@metpolice.uk.

91-year-old man seeks erection. Can you help?

Gay man seeks female for ongoing parental charade.

Narcissistic, masochistic, schizophrenic hypochondriac seeks good listener.

Masochist seeks same for emotional stand-off.

I was the tall, striking redhead on the District Line who got off at Turnham Green, you were the bearded man with the dog, sunglasses and white stick I was blowing kisses at. Call me.

FOR SALE:
binoculars and gloves. Unwanted gifts. Apply Abu Hamza.

Have entire set of *Two Pints of Lager and a Packet of Crisps* DVDs. Will swap for half-eaten can of baked beans. O.N.O.

For the ultimate Australian experience – visit Earl's Court.

WANT A PERSONALISED NUMBER PLATE? VISIT A-R-5-E-O-L-E.CO.UK.

Want a Thai bride? Visit us on nastysurpriseon weddingnight.com.

Buy the Airfix *Diana crash Mercedes* beautiful detailed scale model – complete with Henri Paul hip flask.

WANTED: rubber bedsheet. Apply A. Winehouse.

Keep cats out of your garden with these pressure activated land mines.

Fool burglars with our baked bean tin that's actually a storage box. So realistic, you'll throw it away for recycling and lose your life savings.

Want somewhere to put all your 1p coins? Buy this 1p piggy bank for £10.99.

Finish your series of Christopher Biggins wall-mounted china plates with number five: 'The Rentaghost Years'.

Turn your shoes into fashionable crocks with our exclusive hole puncher.

Here's the ideal present for dads and uncles: a completely trained, fully washable Eastern European au pair.

Feel like Bruce Parry with our one-size-fits-all tribal penis gourd.

WANTED: new iconic female victim for *Daily Express* front page.

Watch how to make thousands quickly with my easy-to-follow course. Send me £1,000 for part one.

Bright copper kettles, warm woollen mittens, brown paper packages tied up with string; 10% off some of your favourite things.

Gillian McKeith's healthy chocolate log with nut and corn, ideal for the Christmas table.

46. LINES YOU WOULDN'T FIND IN A HARRY POTTER BOOK (Part 3)

'Harry,' said Ron awkwardly, 'have you seen *Brokeback Mountain?*'

'I'm afraid your scar has turned malignant, Mr Potter,' said the doctor.

Harry slowly unzipped his trousers...

Harry turned to Tigger and said, 'I'm sorry, I appear to be in the wrong book.'

It wasn't only Harry's feet that stuck out from his cloak of invisibility, as he sneaked into the girls' changing room.

The inspector from Ofsted pulled up outside Hogwarts...

'Imagine that,' said Harry as he stepped out of the shower. 'It was just a dream after all.'

'Once you've had a muggle, you'll never go back,' said Hermione.

Slowly the car carrying J.R.R. Tolkien's literary executor pulled up outside Hogwarts.

Harry tightened the belt around his arm, slapped up a vein and as he injected said, 'Now that is magic.'

Harry had always known he was a woman trapped inside a man's body.

Ron and Harry smiled as the Coventry fans rounded the corner. 'Let's f*cking kill 'em!' they bellowed at their fellow Chelsea Firm members.

'It tastes funny,' Harry heard Hermione say in a muffled voice.

'Shit!' said Ron, as Harry died.

'There's something funny about Professor Hitler...' said Harry.

Hedwig was to be the last owl culled in the wake of the Hogwarts bird-flu scare.

'George Galloway is our new master of the Dark Arts.'

Harry felt Professor Snape's hot breath on the back of his neck.

'This is better than chasing real dragons,' said Harry, as he took the tin foil and rolled-up tenner.

47. QUESTIONS OMITTED FROM THE BRITISH CITIZENSHIP TEST (Part 2)

1. For fast-track applicants: which Premiership club are you most interested in buying?

2. According to the *Daily Mail*, when resident in the UK do you intend to
   a) sponge
   b) cause trouble
   c) refuse to adapt to our bloody culture, or
   d) all of the above?

3. You have a credit card, but you are not in debt. Why not?

4. Last year, a BBC TV trailer portrayed the Queen as a grumpy old cow. In what way was it not telling the truth?

5. Who did put the bomp in the bomp-a-bomp-a bomp, who put the ram in the ram-a-lam-a-ding-dong?

6. What exactly is the wrong sort of snow?

7. Can you speak a foreign language? (A positive answer may not help your case.)

8. It's a sunny Sunday afternoon: what degree skin burns will you have by Monday morning?

9. What is Toad-in-the-Hole, and why?

10. Where is it better to dump an old fridge: on a street corner or in a lay-by?

11. Are either or both of your hands hooks?

12. What word is missing from this sentence: 'The M5 is .... this Bank Holiday Monday'?

13. Which of the queen's children hasn't been divorced?

14. Who is more important in the *Carry On* mythos: Joan Sims or Bernard Bresslaw? Discuss.

15. You're not Mohammed al Fayed, are you?

16. Would you like to donate half a million pounds to the Labour Party? If yes, answer no further questions.

17. Who was better on Basil Brush: Mr Roy or Mr Derek?

18. To the nearest five pounds, how much should you pay for a cup of tea at a service station?

19. For how many weeks of the year are you interested in tennis?

48. QUESTIONS OMITTED FROM THE DRIVING THEORY TEST

1. When cut up at the lights, what is the correct number of fingers to raise?

2. How long after the light turns red are you still allowed to go through it?

3. For how many days can a card saying 'Tax Applied For' be used?

4. Is it ever permissible to swerve into the nearside lane to splash an old lady?

5. True or false: the wing mirror on the passenger side is to see whether you knocked down that cyclist?

6. True or false: 'Bald tyres are sexy.'

7. 'Wee wee wee' or 'woo woo woo' – which of these distinctive car alarm noises will annoy your neighbours most?

8. You are joining a motorway while texting a friend and changing a CD. How do you eat your crisps?

9. In what circumstances can a home-made sign saying 'Doctor on Call' be used?

10. When was the last time you actually put gloves in your glove box?

11. You are taking a corpse to dump in a gravel pit. What is the best way to avoid that incriminating DNA evidence?

12. When leaving your car in a residential area late at night, how do you achieve maximum volume on a door slam?

13. You are driving a white van. Is there any law you need care about?

14. A cyclist is driving the wrong way up a one-way street. Are you allowed to hit him?

15. What the f*ck is this?

16. If cut up by a white van is the correct response a) one finger b) two fingers c) 'w*nker' gesture or d) terrified silence?

17. Does this sign mean:
a) no dogging,
b) beware faulty
electric window or
c) last blow job
for 325 miles?

STOP

95

49. UNFORTUNATE NAMES FOR RACE HORSES (Part 2)

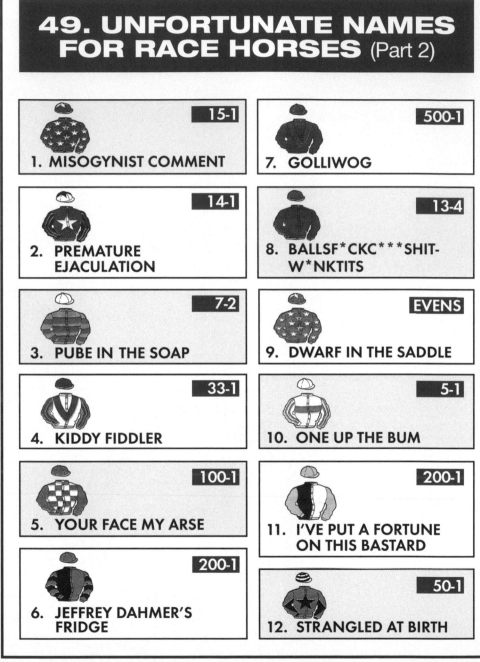

15-1
1. MISOGYNIST COMMENT

14-1
2. PREMATURE EJACULATION

7-2
3. PUBE IN THE SOAP

33-1
4. KIDDY FIDDLER

100-1
5. YOUR FACE MY ARSE

200-1
6. JEFFREY DAHMER'S FRIDGE

500-1
7. GOLLIWOG

13-4
8. BALLSF*CKC***SHIT-W*NKTITS

EVENS
9. DWARF IN THE SADDLE

5-1
10. ONE UP THE BUM

200-1
11. I'VE PUT A FORTUNE ON THIS BASTARD

50-1
12. STRANGLED AT BIRTH

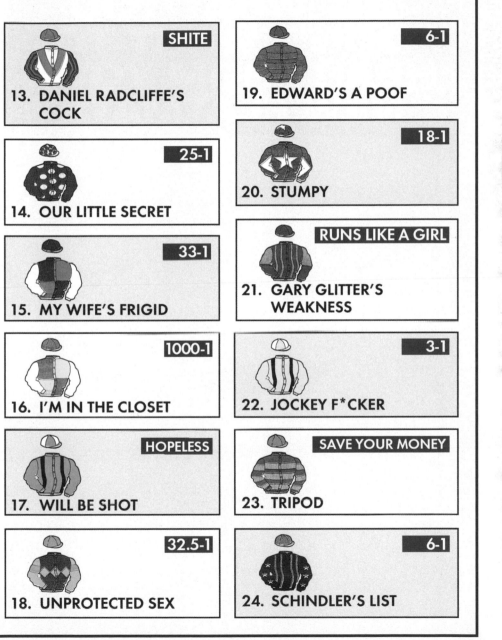

SHITE

13. DANIEL RADCLIFFE'S COCK

25-1

14. OUR LITTLE SECRET

33-1

15. MY WIFE'S FRIGID

1000-1

16. I'M IN THE CLOSET

HOPELESS

17. WILL BE SHOT

32.5-1

18. UNPROTECTED SEX

6-1

19. EDWARD'S A POOF

18-1

20. STUMPY

RUNS LIKE A GIRL

21. GARY GLITTER'S WEAKNESS

3-1

22. JOCKEY F*CKER

SAVE YOUR MONEY

23. TRIPOD

6-1

24. SCHINDLER'S LIST

50. WHAT YOU DON'T WANT TO HEAR FROM YOUR NEW FLATMATE

THIS IS ↗
THE SPECIAL
PEN WE USE
TO MARK
THE MILK

'Throw your tins away, we'll grow all our own food!'

'So I bet you're wondering how I got a nickname like "Fisty"?'

'I've bought some coasters and I'd like you to use them.'

'I don't allow the television after eight o'clock. It interferes with Bible study.'

'I've pinned my allergy list to the kitchen noticeboard and I'd like you to read it very carefully.'

'I'll make supper – I'm boiling your pet bunny.'

'Would you like to see my collection of bird shit?'

'I've invited the Grand Wizard round for supper, Denzil.'

'I'm sorry, did I say torture chamber? I meant "spare room".'

'Don't mind the Civil War helmet – it's for Saturday's re-enactment.'

'If a man called Big Lenny asks where the money is, can you tell him I'm out?'

'I always start the day off with "The Birdie Song" because I'm just crazy!'

'Are you interested in Morris dancing? We're one short.'

'The room's yours until my gran comes to stay – then you'll have to share with her.'

'Now – do you know what hydroponic skunk is?'

'I can't stop now – I'm only halfway through my Eurovision boxset.'

51. FIRST-DRAFT LINES FROM GREAT NOVELS

My father's family name being Pirrip and my Christian name being Philip meant I had a shit time at school.

It is a truth universally acknowledged that a single man in possession of a good fortune must be beating off the pussy with a stick.

It was a bright, cold day in April and the clock struck thirteen. 'Big Ben's on the f*cking blink again,' sighed Winston Smith.

When Mr Bilbo Baggins of Bag End announced that he would shortly be celebrating his eleventy-first birthday, most readers thought 'This sounds shit' and put the book back on the shelf.

It was a dark and stormy night, the rain fell in torrents so I just stayed in and watched telly.

Last night I dreamt I went to Spearmint Rhino again.

'It was the gardener,' said Poirot, 'and over the next 374 pages I will explain how.'

Marley was dead, which was a real pisser for the Wailers.

Call me Ishamel, or u can txt me if u like. Dat wd be betta. Lol Ahab x

'Christmas won't be Christmas without any presents,' grumbled Jo. 'Well tough shit,' said Father, contemplating wrapping the ungrateful little sod up in the rug and setting it on fire.

All children except one grow up. Poor Peter Pan had a congenital kidney disorder, meaning he was stuck at 4ft 3ins.

Lolita, light of my life, bait of my jail.

I am an invisible man and unfortunately, I write in invisible ink.

'Tom!' No answer. 'Tom!' No answer. 'Tom—'
'For f*ck's sake, I'm having a shit!' shouted Tom Sawyer.

As Gregor Samsa awoke one morning, he found himself transformed in his bed into a giant insect. However when he rang work Ken, his line manager, said, 'Right, Samsa, I've had enough of this bollocks: you're fired.'

Alice was beginning to get very bored of sitting by her sister on the riverbank, so she checked no one was around, hit her with a stone and pushed her into the water.

Here is Edward Bear coming downstairs now, bump bump bump on the back of his head behind Christopher Robin. 'Let that be a lesson to you, Edward. Mr Robin doesn't like grasses,' said Christopher.

It was the best of times, yup, it really was the best of times.

Emma Woodhouse was handsome, clever and rich with a comfortable home and happy disposition, but she was gagging for cock.

The drought had lasted for ten million years and the reign of the terrible lizards had long since ended, but still I was in a priority queue and all the operators were busy.

Once upon a time there were four little rabbits: Flopsy, Mopsy, Shagger and Deep Throat.

52. BOOKS HEADED STRAIGHT FOR THE BARGAIN BIN

How to Grow Old with Dignity –
Peter Stringfellow

The Curious Incident of Dogging at Night-time

The A to B of London

The Pop-Up Nude Camilla

Ventriloquism for Dummies

My Struggle – Paris Hilton

Down and Out in Paris Hilton

100 Great Guinea Pig Recipes

Lady Thatcher's Lover

The Rough Guide to Baghdad

Eats, Shoots and Leaves: the Russell Brand
Story

Dennis Potter and the Goblet Of Fire

Pimp My Bookcase

George Best: The Idiotic Drunken Twat

How Clean Is Your Spouse?

Eats, Shoots and Leaves: US Foreign Policy

How to Make the Best of a Death Sentence

How to Get Your Luggage on a Plane

Families and How to Survive Them –
Princess Diana

Stephen Hawking's Deadly Art of
Unarmed Combat

Prince Edward's Guide to Starting a
Small Business

Shag Yourself Thin – John Prescott

Pete Doherty's Scratch 'n' Sniff

How to Write a Postcard – a Step By Step Guide
(Volume I)

100 Great Tube Journeys

Raising Flies

Lizards of Wales

John Betjeman's Sex Life in Pictures

Drainspotting

Roy Keane's Little Book of Calm

I Did it My Way – Tord Grip

53. REJECTED NAMES FOR ROYAL NAVY SHIPS

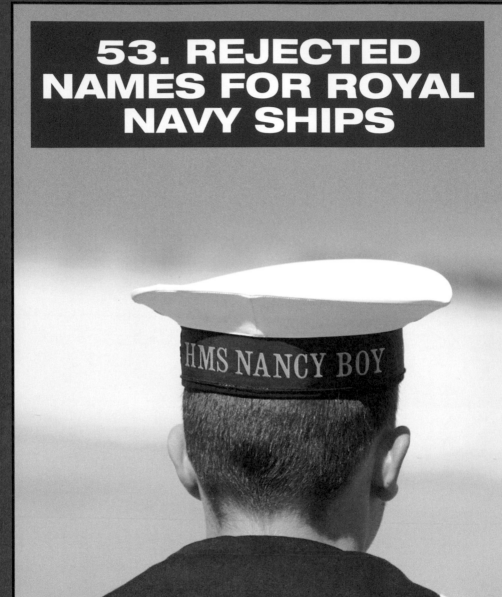

HMS SMITHEREENS

HMS PATRICIA ROUTLEDGE

HMS FRIENDLY FIRE

HMS CHLAMYDIA

HMS POSEIDON

HMS SKIMPED ON MATERIALS

HMS PEDALO

HMS AGROUND

HMS GIRL

HMS TOUCHY FEELY

HMS RECYCLABLE

HMS BUGGERY

HMS GLUG-GLUG-GLUG

HMS PHALLUS

HMS COMPROMISE

HMS TAMPON

HMS VULNERABLE

HMS BARBARA STREISAND

HMS RETARDED

HMS BUTTF*CK

HMS FLIMSY

HMS MACRAMÉ

HMS BAMBI

HMS L'ORÉAL

HMS ICEBERG

HMS PANIC

HMS DILDO

HMS NETBALL

HMS PORNOGRAPHIC

HMS PEA-GREEN BOAT

HMS JUMBLY

HMS LEAKING

HMS ROBINSON CRUSOE

HMS GRAHAM NORTON

HMS NOT A LOT OF LIFEBOATS, SORRY

HMS DROWNING

HMS SHIT-TIP

HMS CUTBACKS

HMS ABYSS

HMS SOMME

HMS ANUSOL

HMS COWARDICE

HMS LOVE BOAT

HMS FLOATING CEMETERY

HMS ECRET SERVICE

HMS COLANDER

54. BAD THINGS TO SEE OR HEAR AT A HOTEL (Part 1)

'Welcome to the Hotel California, you can check out any time you like but you'll never leave.'

'Welcome to the Hotel Towering Inferno.'

'Five stars ... is what you can see through the holes in the ceiling.'

'We have a 24-hour room service and a 24-hour mysterious buzzing and clanging sound you'll be unable to stop.'

'The chef is one of the most sought-after in Europe but INTERPOL have no idea he is here.'

'Yes, you're in the Darfur suite.'

'Well, interestingly, Oscar Wilde is amongst the hundreds of people that have died in that room.'

'The sheets are yellow deliberately to cover the stains.'

'Each room contains heated towel rail, hairdryer, TV and a large two-way mirror through which you will be filmed by the hotel staff.'

Hotel Policy

DRUG ADDICTS, PROSTITUTES AND ILLEGAL IMMIGRANTS WELCOME

The Management

55. LINES YOU WON'T FIND IN THE BIBLE (Part 2)

To be continued.

And the Lord did summon to him as his followers James and his brother John, and Simon who is called 'Duckie'.

And the customers did return with their tables and chairs and said unto Jesus, 'This furniture is of shoddy quality.'

And lo, at the wedding feast the wine was all consumed and Jesus did take the jugs of water and spake unto his disciples, 'You'll like this, but not a lot.'

File under 'Fiction'.

And many Polish carpenters did appear in the land of Judea and did price the Lord out of business.

Here beginneth the Gospel according to Dan Brown...

And Jesus did walk in the wilderness for forty days and forty nights before finally asking someone, 'Which aisle for household goods, please?'

Any resemblance to any characters dead or alive is purely coincidental.

IF YOU TAKE THE FIRST LETTER OF EVERY SENTENCE IN GENESIS, IT SPELLS OUT 'THE DA VINCI CODE'.

OTHER RELIGIONS ARE AVAILABLE.

THOU SHALT NOT READ OUT ANY BITS ON AMERICAN TELEVISION AND ASK FOR MONEY.

AND THEY ALL LIVED HAPPILY EVER AFTER. THE END.

HE WHO TURNS ANY PART OF THIS INTO A MUSICAL SHALL BE CURSED WITH A DISFIGURED FACE.

THE WISE MEN CAME FROM THE EAST. AND THE FOOLISH MAN CAME ON NETWORK SOUTH-EAST, AND ARRIVED ON THE 27TH.

EVERYTHING I'M SAYING IS GOOD FOR TWO THOUSAND YEARS, UNTIL RICHARD DAWKINS GETS HERE.

CAN YOU CHANGE IT BACK TO WATER AGAIN, MATE? I'M DRIVING.

I'M SURE WE HAD TWO OF EVERYTHING, MRS NOAH – NOT JUST TWO FAT LIONS.

JESUS JESUS, GIVE US A WAVE!

ABOUT THE AUTHOR: GOD LIVES AND WORKS EVERYWHERE. HE HAS ONE SON. THIS IS HIS FIRST BOOK.

ETERNAL LIFE IS NOT GUARANTEED AND MAY DEPEND ON PAST PERFORMANCE; YOUR SOUL MAY GO DOWN AS WELL AS UP.

56. POOR SUGGESTIONS FOR NEW OLYMPIC EVENTS

Fig 1:

GRECO-ROMAN FOREPLAY

4x100M SHIT

HOP, SKIP AND MINCE

THE 3000M PEOPLECHASE

BREASTSTROKE IN PYJAMAS WHILE CARRYING
A BRICK

HUNTING WITH JAVELINS

RHYTHMIC SEXUAL INTERCOURSE

SPEED CRAPPING

OLD-FASHIONED PENTATHLON

BOLLOCK-NAKED VOLLEYBALL

CROSS-COUNTRY STREAKING

HAPPY SLAPPING

DRIVE-BY RIFLE SHOOTING

EGG AND SPOON RACE

SYNCHRONISED FLASHING

CROSS-CHANNEL BOOZING

SHIT PUT

LONG DUMP

HIGH PISS

57. WALLCHARTS THE PAPERS DIDN'T GIVE AWAY (Part 1)

PENCIL STRENGTHS

PEOPLE WHO WENT TO SCHOOL WITH MY MUM

ENVELOPE SIZES

MINISTERS FOR AGRICULTURE

GAY SEX PRACTICES

BURNS VICTIMS

GOITRES

FAMOUS IN-THE-CLOSET HOMOSEXUALS

LOVERS OF THE DUKE OF EDINBURGH

SPERM

VICTIMS OF FRED AND ROSE WEST

THE GUNS OF NAVARONE

LETTERS OF THE ALPHABET

58. DISCARDED ADVERTISING SLOGANS
(Part 3)

OWN BRAND SAUSAGES – WHO'D HAVE THOUGHT AN ARSEHOLE COULD TASTE SO GOOD?

JUST BECAUSE I'M WEARING OVERALLS AND A BADGE SAYING 'CAN I HELP YOU?', IT DOESN'T MEAN I CAN HELP YOU

EXCLUSIVELY WITH THE DAILY MAIL, A FANTASTIC FREE DVD – OF A LONG-FORGOTTEN AMERICAN MINI-SERIES THAT EVERYONE HATED AT THE TIME

KILLS 99% OF ALL KNOWN GERMS – LEAVING THE DEADLY 1% STILL ALIVE

STOP CRYING AND SAYING YOU'RE MISSING YOUR MUMMY, THOSE TRAINERS NEED STITCHING, JUST DO IT

BUY A 4X4 AND STUFF THE PLANET – COS THE KIDS SHOULDN'T HAVE TO WALK A HUNDRED YARDS TO SCHOOL

FOR MASH, GET POTATOES

LADYSHAVE – THE BEST A CLAM CAN GET

SPECIAL-STRENGTH LAGER – ENJOY IT IN YOUR FAVOURITE PARK OR ALLEYWAY

CADBURY'S CREME EGGS — HOW DO YOU REGURGITATE YOURS?

'MUMMY, WHY ARE YOUR HANDS SO SOFT?'
'BECAUSE THAT NICE BULGARIAN GIRL DOES THE WASHING UP'

TIRED OF THE SAME OLD PORN?

IT'S NOT JUST HAEMORRHOID CREAM, IT'S LIP GLOSS TOO!

TAKE TWO RENT BOYS INTO THE SHOWER?

HOW MANY TIMES HAVE YOU THOUGHT, 'I WISH I HADN'T SHAGGED THAT GOAT?'

HI, I'M THE PRESIDENT OF IRAN, AND I LIKED RUSSIAN URANIUM SO MUCH THAT I BOUGHT THE COMPANY

HI, I'M ROBERT MUGABE, AND I'M HERE TO TALK TO YOU ABOUT INDIGESTION RELIEF

THIS BEAUTIFUL SOFA LOOKS LOVELY, DOESN'T IT? BUT IT WON'T LOOK HALF AS GOOD IN YOUR CRAMPED FRONT ROOM

OUR NEW ULTRA-HIGH-FIBRE BRAN CEREAL WILL GO THROUGH WITHOUT TOUCHING THE SIDES!

BUDGETAIR — WE'RE THE CHEAPEST, BECAUSE WE DON'T GIVE A SHIT ABOUT YOU OR ANYTHING

59. THINGS YOU'LL NEVER READ ON FACEBOOK

All your friends are now zombies … they're everywhere, run, hide, we're doomed!

You have been poked by Russell Brand.

You have been invited to Michael Barrymore's pool party.

Al-Qaeda has sent you a present.

You have 0 friends.

Gordon Brown is undecided over whether to become your friend.

Amy Winehouse has bought you a drink.

Lord Lucan has updated his status.

Cliff Richard is now married.

Janette Krankie has posted new pictures in the album 'Me: Fan-dabby-naked!'

Banksy has written on your wall.

Max Mosley has tagged you in a video.

Looking up www.bbc.co.uk...

Thu 19:37

Google

Settings ▾

Gordon Brown has left the group 'Let's scrap the 10p tax band'.

Sir Alex Ferguson has accepted a friendship request from the BBC.

Sir Paul McCartney has changed his relationship status to 'Phew!'

Robert Mugabe has joined the group 'I bet I can find another 10,000,000 people to vote in the Zimbabwe general election'.

Sarah Beeny is NOT pregnant.

A loner has sent you a suspect package.

Osama bin Laden is in Croydon.

Can you confirm these details:

We met randomly and had an adulterous one-night stand.

We were part of the web community Paedoheaven.co.uk.

We worked together smuggling drugs out of Thailand.

We lived together in the maximum security wing at Broadmoor Hospital.

60. SURPRISING THINGS TO READ ON A LABEL (Part 2)

CHICKEN

INGREDIENTS:

SALMONELLA **70%**
WATER **30%**

	06JUN		07JUN	
Display until			Use by	
£/lb	1.49	£ **6.05**	3.29	£/kg
UK 2037 EC			**1.840** kg	

'Made in Great Britain'

'Hand-stitched by Abu Hamza'

'Parental guidance – you will be more offended than your children'

'Highly flammable – or do I mean inflammable? Oh God, I never know the difference'

'Best before yesterday'

'Turkey cooking time: two hours longer than you expect'

'Serves two – if you're not very hungry'

'Size 14 (size 4 after a wash)'

'Caution: may contain nuts, milk or wheat, you sad allergic bastards'

'Contains wheat, gluten, soya, barley and free choking hazard'

'Gourmet crisps – just how much will you pay for one potato?'

On a copy of *The Beginner's Guide to Conmen*: 'Special One for Two Offer!'

61. HOW NOT TO END A NEWS BULLETIN

'I don't know why you're pretending to shuffle your papers, Bert.'

'And on a lighter note, Fluffy the cat today unearthed… a severed human head.'

'You couldn't make this shit up, could you?'

'On a personal note, I'm much too good for this.'

'And the missiles are on their way over to us as I speak… just kidding.'

'And the main points of the news again: blah blah blah.'

' … Arsenal 0 … ha ha! Suck on that, Arsène!'

'And now, the end is near, and so I face the final curtain…'

'And now over to Susan for the weather … There's no whether about it, I definitely would.'

'Personally, I think they should drop Harmison and bring in Stuart Broad; at least he can bat.'

'Shit, that was my f*cking street flooded there, everything will be ruined – my new carpet!'

'And in other news: my contract ends in a fortnight if you're watching, Sky.'

'That's it from a news bulletin that runs as smoothly as a Peugeot 307 from Ted Collins Motors of Lowestoft. They're great.'

'The Queen there, still pretty hot for 82, I think you'll agree.'

'The case is continuing, but if any members of the jury are watching, I think we know what the verdict is going to be, don't we?'

'This bloke did this thing.'

'Right, tonight I'm going to improvise. Now can someone give me an accent I can read it in, "Chinese" is the first one I heard…'

'And now tonight's lottery numbers: 3, 7, 34… wooohooooo!!! I'm outtahere!'

'I read the news today, oh boy.'

'It's goodnight from me and it's goodnight from him.'

62. GREETINGS CARDS THAT WOULDN'T SELL (Part 3)

To a very special stepson by my second marriage, on the occasion of your gay wedding

Sorry you failed your driving test. See you at the pedestrian's funeral

Happy 143rd Birthday

Sorry for your very sad loss. Who's getting his laptop?

Congratulations on your first affair! Pay a hundred quid to this address or the photos go public

Happy Birthday, Sweet Sixteen – you can now wear this badge: 'I'm Legal'

Sorry to hear you're dead

Happy Anniversary! Who'd have thought it's a year since your family were all killed in that tragic accident?

Thank you for that night of passion. I think I've given you chlamydia

Congratulations on your divorce. I never liked him

Commiserations, you've got breast/testicular/prostate cancer (delete as appropriate)

63. UNSUCCESSFUL JOB APPLICATIONS

I love all animals, especially with mustard.

I won't travel.

Deer Surr or Madum...

I am both lazy and a miserable git.

Cell 6, HMP Pentonville, London.

Qualifications: 7 ASBOs, endorsed driving licence, restraining order.

I am an ambitious, motivated, rampant homosexual.

I have a phobia of desks and computers.

I worked as a web designer on the now defunct sites 'LustyLolitas.com' and 'UnderagePussy. co.uk'.

It has always been my dream to work as a sandwich maker in Subway.

Name: Sutcliffe, Peter
Job history: 1977-1981 Lorry driver.
1981-2008: errm, doing A levels, I now have 113.
I like to set myself goals and never fail to miss.

I have attention deficit disorder, Tourette's, body odour and love dogging.

I have just come back from a 23-year senten-
sorry, spell in Vietnam.

I would like to work for your company to pay the
bills and hopefully use colleagues for casual
sex until I find a better-paid and more enjoyable
position.

I am an ambitious, conscientious, hardworking,
curvy blonde who is up for anything.

I don't work well on my own or as part of a group.

I like to see myself as a 'people person'; others
use the term 'rapist'.

I worked as a strategist for Northern Rock, Enron
and Mayor Ken's campaign team.

Employers 2001–2006: Al Qaeda.
Reference: Mr O. bin Laden, Cave 6, Jihad Road,
Kandahar, Afghanistan.

My name is Steve McClaren and I would love to be
manager of your international football team.

I would be ideal for the vacancy at your company
because I have not worked since 1976.

I have considerable experience working with
spazzers.

Gizza job, go on, I can do that.

64. DVDS THAT WOULDN'T SELL

Accident at Work – Uncut!

Gordon Brown: The Collected Speeches

Great British Diabetics

John McCririck's Lover's Guide

Live and Dangerous: The Best of the M6 Contraflows

Music and Lyrics – the Director's Cut

Naked Pilates with Vanessa Feltz

My Greatest Goals, *by Gary Neville*

DIY Colonic Irrigation with Michael Winner

Tracing Your Family Tree, with Prince Harry

Juggling in Three Easy Steps, with Abu Hamza

Pylons of Britain

Helen Mirren and Judi Dench in Yet Another Bloody Film

Celebrity Wrestling: the Complete Series 1 *box set*

Antiques Roadshow: Too Hot for TV!

Clarissa Dickson-Wright's Tae Kwondo

The Pope, Live and Lewd

Celebrity Love Island: the Over-80s

Lifestyles of the Poor and Obscure

Britain's Beautiful Laundrettes

Ready Steady Sleep

Cambridge United: The Glory Years

Pauline, Sue and Prescott Too

Rocky 12: The Fight Against Incontinence

Richard Curtis's **Apocalypse Now**

The Complete Webcameron Season 1

Nude Footballers' Wives: Lady Stanley Matthews meets Joy Beverley

No Holds Barred Origami

Regional Weather – Uncut!

The Queen's Speech – Too Hot for TV!

Thirty Years of Direct Line Insurance Ads

65. UNLIKELY ADDRESSES

DOGGERS'
MEADOWS

THE HAROLD SHIPMAN REST HOME

HINDENBERG AIRPORT

PAEDOPHILE PARK

THE WAYNE ROONEY REST HOME

THE KATE GARRAWAY DANCE ACADEMY

AVENUE OF THE NAZIS

THE CHARLES KENNEDY HEALTHY LIVING CLINIC

RED LIGHT CRESCENT

THE PHIL NEVILLE SCHOOL OF EXCELLENCE

RAPISTS' LANE

THE TORD GRIP STAND

THE JEREMY CLARKSON ALTERNATIVE ENERGY
CENTRE

PETER SUTCLIFFE HIGH SCHOOL

STEVE McCLAREN WAY

JADE GOODY COLLEGE

GENOCIDE SQUARE

SALMAN RUSHDIE STREET

TAMPAX STADIUM

66. MUSICALS THAT DIDN'T MAKE IT TO BROADWAY

ALL THAT JIZZ

SEVEN BRIDES FOR SEVEN SISTERS

SEVEN ARRANGED MARRIAGES FOR SEVEN BROTHERS

SEVEN BRIDES FOR SEVEN CHUCKLE BROTHERS

AN AMERICAN IN PARIS HILTON

GO WEST: THE FRED AND ROSE STORY

CORGI AND BESS: THE STORY OF QUEEN ELIZABETH II AND ONE OF HER DOGS

HEATHER MILLS IN ... *FOOTLOOSE*

THE WOMAN IN WHITE, THE WOMAN IN BLACK, FOR GOD'S SAKE, WOMAN, WE'VE GOT TO BE THERE AT EIGHT

DOGS

WEARSIDE STORY

LES HAPPY

PIMP YOUR WAGON

ROOFER ON THE FIDDLE

PIRATE VIDEOS OF PENZANCE

GAYS AND DOLLS

RYVITA

CHITTY CHITTY GANG BANG

FRANK SINATRA AND GENE KELLY IN *ON THE PISS*

PAINT YOUR WOGAN

JAILHOUSE COCK

THE SOUND OF MUCUS

JOSEPH AND HIS AMAZING AMOUNT OF FREE PUBLICITY ON BBC 1 PRIMETIME

MEET ME IN ST HELENS

PAEDO OF THE OPERA

THE JOCKY WILSON PICTURE SHOW

ANNIE GET YOUR ASBO

GREASY

THOROUGHLY MODERN MILIBAND

67. UNLIKELY HOROSCOPES

 PISCES
Feb 21 – March 20
Hitler will invade Poland in 1939.

 ARIES
March 21 – April 20
You will see a man, or possibly a woman, unless you don't leave the house maybe.

 TAURUS
Apr 21 – May 21
Like your star sign, Taurus, this is bull.

GEMINI
May 22 – Jun 22
A stranger will come into your midst and cause an accident or expire at your feet (this applies only to people who live in the TV programme *Casualty*).

 CANCER
June 23 – July 23
Soon Cancer won't just be your star sign.

 LEO
July 24 – Aug 23
You will regret having wasted 45 pence and about twenty seconds of your day any time around about ... now, there you go, told you.

 VIRGO
Sept 24 – Oct 23
The letter you are expecting will be late.

 SCORPIO
Oct 24 – Nov 22
The winning lottery numbers will be 7, 9, 17, 24, 29 and 33, though this may be a week out of date.

SAGITTARIUS
Nov 23 – Dec 21
All Sagittarians are c**ts.

 CAPRICORN
Dec 22 – Jan 20
Is this the card you were thinking of?

AQUARIUS
Jan 21 – Feb 19
You are being fooled by an overpaid charlatan who started out as a sports reporter, but realised where the real money is.

PISCES
Feb 21 – March 20
You will meet a dark stranger today, particularly if you live in Africa.

ARIES
March 21 – April 20
You are a closet homosexual.

TAURUS
Apr 21 – May 21
You should go to your bedroom window and stand there naked for a minute, then turn around and stay there for another minute, you should do this especially if your name is Mrs Hughes and you live at 56, The Avenue, Clapham ... around 3.30 would be best for me.

GEMINI
May 22 – Jun 22
Mercury is prominent today, so don't drink tap water.

CANCER
June 23 – July 23
You are about to have a brilliant week, but after reading this you will remember nothing.

LEO
July 24 – Aug 23
Look out for an old lady on a zebra crossing this morning ... oops, too late.

VIRGO
Sept 24 – Oct 23
There is a gun trained on you, Virgo; now stay still, don't try anything and no one will get hurt, understand?

SCORPIO
Oct 24 – Nov 22
Today you will feel much better/ worse [delete as applicable]

SAGITTARIUS
Nov 23 – Dec 21
You are a gullible person.

68. ILL-ADVISED NAMES FOR MILITARY OPERATIONS

OPERATION CLUELESS

OPERATION NO HOPE

OPERATION WASTE OF YOUNG LIFE

OPERATION QUAGMIRE

OPERATION CREAM PUFF

OPERATION HORRIFIC BLOODBATH

OPERATION DIDN'T THEY USED TO BE OUR FRIENDS?

OPERATION ILL-THOUGHT OUT

OPERATION CAN OF WORMS

OPERATION RUN LIKE F★CK

OPERATION DENGUE FEVER

OPERATION WE CAN BUT TRY

OPERATION DESSERT SPOON

OPERATION I'M OUT OF HERE

OPERATION WHAT, IN THERE? AGAINST THEM?

OPERATION F★CKWITS

OPERATION LOOSE BOWELS

OPERATION GALLIPOLI

OPERATION LEMMING

OPERATION ONE THING AFTER ANOTHER

69. UNAPPETISING THINGS TO READ ON A MENU (Part 3)

Thai Soup – chicken, pork, shrimp or baby seal

Mexican-style main course*: burrito, enchilada or taco (*includes amoebic dysentery)

Prawn à la Sewer

A selection of steaks ruined on our barbecue

Cooked either well done, medium, medium rare or dripping with warm life, blood still pulsing through its twitching, pain-wracked cadaver

Duck au Ketchup

Fresh peaches in lard

All our chickens were force fed for two months in a cage too small to stand up in

We're obviously overcharging so just pay what you want

All our beef has been humanely shot with a bolt gun, piled in huge stacks, lightly doused in accelerant and set alight by fully trained men in masks

70. THE WORST RECORDS IN THE WORLD ... EVER! (Part 1)

THE CATHOLIC BISHOPS' CHOIR

SIDE A
45 RPM CATHB 1690
Made in the Vatican

'MAD ABOUT THE BOY'

★ IAN HUNTLEY SINGS...

★ THE COMPLETE HARRY POTTER READ BY PROFESSOR STEPHEN HAWKING

★ ANN WIDDECOMBE'S 'JE T'AIME'

★ PRINCES WILLIAM AND HARRY: 'THERE'S NO ONE QUITE LIKE GRANDMA'

★ THE LOVE BALLADS OF CRADLE OF FILTH

★ IAIN DUNCAN SMITH'S GREATEST SPEECHES

★ KARAOKE FOR THE DEAF

★ NOW THAT'S WHAT I CALL MIME

★ 20 FUNERAL SINGALONG HITS

★ 'YOU'LL NEVER W*NK ALONE'

★ 'YOU'RE ONCE, TWICE, THREE TIMES OVER THE LEGAL LIMIT'

★ 'A DAY IN THE WIFE'

71. TERRIBLE PICK-UP LINES

'I'm having it cut off tomorrow, so think of it as a sort of farewell voyage.'

'Would you like to see my penis?'

'That's just the psoriasis.'

'Come on, luv, I only need a Kraut for the full set.'

'So, how long have you been doing your own conveyancing?'

'Just stand slightly to the left, I'm trying to hide my stiffy.'

'It comes off at the knee, see?'

'Now are you definitely sixteen? Once bitten, twice shy and all that.'

'Hello. I'm Michael Winner.'

'Have you ever been to a Harvester before?'

'Do you mind inserting my enema?'

'You look ugly enough to be prepared to f*ck me.'

'Mum, can I sleep in your bed tonight?'

'My cock's on Myspace.'

'I'm Barry Scott, let's try a Cillit Bang.'

'Your sister was shit.'

'Would you like to see my puppetry of the anus?'

'How much for the whole night?'

'Hold me pint, I'm just going for a dump.'

'It's in there somewhere, have a good rummage, I know, it's like a needle in a bloody haystack.'

'Put this bag on your head will you, luv?'

'Well if I shag you and your dad, I've done all the family.'

'Have you got herpes as well?'

'You're even more beautiful than my cock.'

'What are your views on a European single currency?'

'How would you like to come home and squat over my coffee table?'

'You remind me of my daughter.'

'Oh sorry, is this the ladies'? Force of habit.'

'I felt sorry for you so thought I'd come over and say hello.'

'Oh go on, I've only got 48 hours to live.'

'Have you eaten? Well get your mouth round this.'

'Wrap me in your bingo wings.'

'You are either a beautiful man or a really ugly woman…'

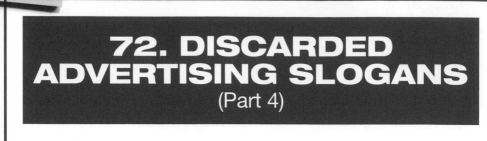

72. DISCARDED ADVERTISING SLOGANS
(Part 4)

DO PEOPLE LAUGH AT YOUR PENIS?

WALKERS CRISPS – PUTTING ALL THE OTHER CRISP COMPANIES OUT OF BUSINESS

PAMPERS NAPPIES – WE'RE FULL OF SHIT

HAVE YOU GOT A CLEAN LICENCE AND FIVE YEARS' NO CLAIMS BONUS? THEN YOU'LL GET A GOOD DEAL FROM ANYBODY, YOU CERTAINLY DON'T NEED US

TREAT YOURSELF TO A DUCHY ORIGINAL BISCUIT – ALL PROFITS GO TOWARDS CURING MY WIFE'S DISTEMPER

DROPPING THE KIDS OFF AT THE EX-WIFE'S? THEN PACK 'EM FULL OF LEMONADE AND BUY A DRUM KIT

I'M BEING PAID A FORTUNE TO ADVERTISE THIS SHAMPOO, BUT I'M NOT WORTH IT

DRINK ONE BOTTLE OF THIS AND YOU'LL BE AS FUNNY AS THE MAN IN THE ADVERTS; DRINK TEN AND YOU'LL BE VOMITING IN THE GUTTER

THIS EXCITING NEW FIVE-LITRE SPORTS CAR – WILL GET YOU BANNED IN 4.6 SECONDS

ARE YOU STARTING TO GET WRINKLES? WELL, YOU'RE BOUND TO AT YOUR AGE

THE BRITISH ARMY – BE ALL THAT YOU CAN BE: AN AMPUTEE WITH SHELL SHOCK

THE BEST A MAN CAN GET IS TWIN SISTERS AND A GRAM OF COCAINE. SOD SHAVING

DRINK OUR SPRING WATER, FILTERED THROUGH ROCK FOR THOUSANDS OF YEARS. BEST BEFORE NOVEMBER

CHOCOLATE ORANGE: TAP IT, UNWRAP IT, MAKE YOURSELF SICK

TODAY IN YOUR SUPER SOARAWAY SUN: READ SOME MADE-UP BOLLOCKS ABOUT A SHARK THEN HAVE A CRAFTY WANK OVER PAGE 3

'PAPA'
'NICOLE!'
'PAPA, DON'T TOUCH ME THERE'

RUGGED 4X4 OFF-ROAD VEHICLE: STUFF THE ENVIRONMENT, YOU WON'T SPILL YOUR TEA WHEN YOU GO OVER A SPEED-BUMP

'I'M JAMIE OLIVER – WHY NOT EAT TOO MUCH FOOD, LIKE I DO?'

HOW MANY TIMES A DAY DO YOU THINK, 'I WISH I DIDN'T SMELL OF ROTTING MEAT?'

73. WALLCHARTS THE PAPERS DIDN'T GIVE AWAY (Part 2)

VITAL BRITISH MILITARY SECRETS

STARS OF THE UNIBOND LEAGUE

STOOL SAMPLES

WEATHER PRESENTERS OF THE TYNE-TEES REGION

STARS OF THE SEX OFFENDERS REGISTER

PEBBLES OF THE WORLD

THE SPECTACLES OF JOHN MAJOR

ROYAL AUTOPSIES

CONKERS

THE AL-QAEDA HIT LIST

BRITISH NEWSPAPERS' FREE WALLCHARTS

BIRD EXCREMENT

THE DULUX COLOUR CHART

GREAT BRITISH MILITARY FIGURES

THE GRAND OLD DUKE OF YORK'S MEN

continues overleaf

74. THEATRE REVIEWS YOU'LL NEVER SEE

"This is a load of shit."

"Vanessa Feltz is pure theatrical Viagra."

"Mug someone for a ticket – NOW – stab them ... him there, he'll do..."

"Darren Day IS King Lear."

"You'll see a cock and some bush and a bit of tit."

"*James Blunt: The Musical* is a triumph."

"If you're a poof, you'll love this."

"*We Will Rock You*, starring Barry George."

"*Equus* – your chance to see Harry Potter's cock."

"Crash Bang Wallop! What a f*cking nightmare, I've dropped my laptop."

"You'll believe a man can walk out after five minutes and ask for his money back."

"It moved me to tears ... it was so boring."

"*The Vagina Monologues* is a worldwide phenomenon, having starred the likes of Kate Winslet, Jerry Hall, Whoopi Goldberg and Sharon Stone. Now it comes to your town with, err ... Jenny Éclair and Marlene from *Only Fools and Horses*."

"New *Chitty Chitty Bang Bang* – you'll believe a car can fly and that people can't act."

"Peter Sutcliffe is a revelation."

"From the makers of *Miss Saigon* comes: *Miss Darfur*."

"Abu Hamza is the best fiddler since Topol."

"*The Paula Radcliffe Story* will run and run."

"I masturbated all the way through."

"I couldn't stop crying when I realised how much I paid for this ticket."

"As the Tiger devoured Roy, you could hear the audience stunned by the duo's stagecraft..."

"Ronnie Corbett is a bold choice to play Othello."

"What *Mamma Mia* did for Abba, this will do for anal sex."

75. UNLIKELY MEDICAL LABELS (Part 2)

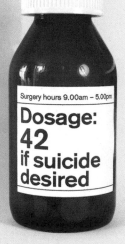

Surgery hours 9.00am – 5.00pm

Dosage:
42
if suicide
desired

May cause unconsciousness in that girl you fancy at the bar, but you didn't hear it from us, OK?

May cause diarrhoea, dysentery, flatulence, piles and other hilarious bottom-related ailments.

Do not attempt to pick on someone bigger and tougher than you.

Warning: may lead to growing an extra limb or, in extreme cases, two heads.

Should not be taken ironically.

May kill or cause you to kill others.

Do not give to children unless they are really pissing you off.

Do not take if breathing.

May cause homosexuality.

Do not admit to taking if trying to impress someone.

Swallow pill, count to ten, breathe out, fingers crossed.

Do not become addicted to … oops, too late.

Keep away from small children, you paedo.

Do not stop thinking about tomorrow.

Store in a cool, dry place if you know of anywhere, which I doubt.

Children: 1 tablet daily; adults: 3 tablets daily; Amy Winehouse: 34 tablets immediately.

Warning: don't say we didn't warn you.

If you have been prescribed these, it's probably already too late.

Smear onto testicles, not necessarily your own.

Warning: has no effect other than making you think something is helping in the last few, miserable days of your existence.

For best results, take when not ill.

76. LINES YOU'D NEVER SEE IN A JAMES BOND BOOK (Part 1)

'We're very proud of this little gadget, it means you can plug things in all over Europe,' beamed Q.

Bond looked into the Austrian's eyes. 'Your go,' Stumpf said coldly, confident he had won games like this, in casinos like this, against men like Bond a million times. A bead of sweat formed on Bond's lip as he made his move with an affected nonchalance. 'Snap,' he said, and lit a cigarette.

Groaning and exhausted, Bond summoned his last strength and released one hand from behind his back, moving it with practised ease to the packet of Rennie's in his pocket.

Fighting his fatigue, Bond pressed a button on his keyboard. His heart pounded as the message came up: 'Goldfinger has added you as a friend on Facebook'.

'He may not look like much, Bond, but he's got a sharp, poisoned implant in his cock, so don't let him f*ck you.'

'That's funny,' said Bond wistfully. 'My mother's name was Pussy Galore too.'

Bond eased out of his Kappa tracksuit bottoms, removed his Burberry baseball cap and placed his Aquascutum jumper on the bed. He was alone in his apartment and enjoying catching up with Britain's Hardest Pubs on Sky One over a 'chow mein' Pot Noodle.

77. UNLIKELY CROSSWORD CLUES (Part 2)

8   **9**

16   **17**   **18**

19

20   **21**

22

ACROSS

1   Cabinet minister and in-the-closet homosexual who tied me up and bummed me (6, 7)

8   Presenter of *Tonight with Jay Leno* (3,4)

9   Dyke, doughnut basher, rug muncher, bean flicker etc. (7)

9   My mum's maiden name (7)

10   One of the letters of the alphabet (1)

11   Who you should vote for in the next election (5, 7)

13   Type of 16th-century Dutch drinking vessel that only four people now living have heard of (7)

16   Not small – rhymes with pig (3)

17   Just fill in the blanks to look clever (9, 12)

20   Apricot knee Simon – well a nun might if the Zeppelin has grown its own Byzantium (16, 8)

21   Slang for female genital area or Russell Brand (4)

22   Greek god invented by crossword compilers (8)

78. COMPUTER GAMES THAT WOULDN'T SELL (Part 2)

Gareth Batty Cricket

True Crime: Streets of Chipping Sodbury

Charles Manson's Killing Spree – Rated 12

Guitar Saddo 3

*Wii F*ck*

Grand Fraud Electoral 4

Alan Titchmarsh Garden Master

Street Cleaner II

World of Handicraft

Boris Goes Cycling

Super Mario Bros vs HM Inland Revenue and Customs

Bang Bang Yawn Yawn

Virtua Town Planner

Pro-Evolution Creationist

Have You Been Outside Today?

Self Assessment Tax 8

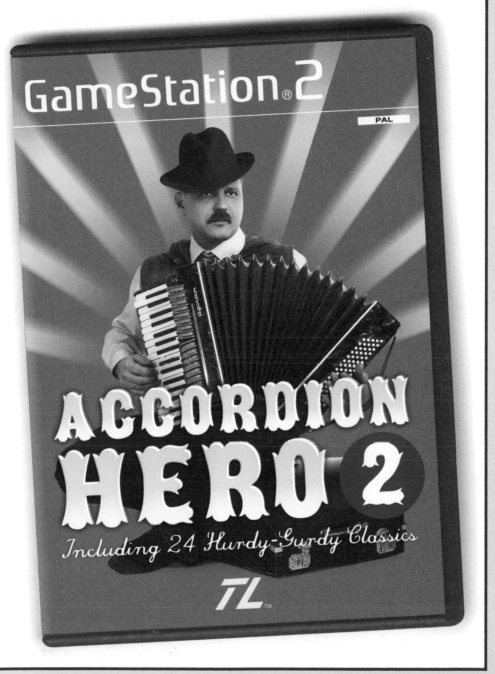

79. UNFORTUNATE CAR NUMBER PLATES

GB SHITDRVR

GB PIG CAR

GB 5UI CIDE

GB 5PEEDIN

GB 5TO LEN

GB AR5E

GB NA21 55

GB 5TOP M3

GB 5TILL 15

GB NO MOT

GB NOT 5EXI

GB COKSUKR

80. THE WORST RECORDS IN THE WORLD ... EVER! (Part 2)

45 RPM

SIDE A

EYE OF THE TIGER
THE CHINESE HERBAL MEDICINE CHOIR

Fu Manchu Records FOO 417
Made in China

★ 'I LEFT MY HAT IN SAN FRANCISCO'

★ 'I WON'T SURVIVE'

★ 'RSPCA'

★ 'CAESAREAN RHAPSODY'

★ 'BUGGERED FOR THE VERY FIRST TIME'

★ 'YOU'VE LOST THAT LIVIN' FEELING'

★ 'YOU'VE GOT TO HIDE YOUR PORN AWAY'

★ 'YOU STOLE MY SON FROM MY CAR'

★ 'SHITE CHRISTMAS'

★ 'WHEREVER I LAY MY HAT (THAT'S USUALLY
WHERE IT IS WHEN I COME BACK)'

★ 'ANARCHY IN THE AA'

★ 'WHO'S THAT C**T?'

★ 'JUMPING JACK FLASHER'

81. BAD THINGS TO SEE OR HEAR AT A HOTEL (Part 2)

'Welcome to the Hotel Pestilence.'

'Are you here for the royal sex video? Room 314.'

'Would you like a prostitute in the morning, Sir?'

'We do have an alternative room, 617, it's in between the Sarah Harding and Pete Doherty parties.'

'How would you like your E. coli?'

'What floor would you like your child thrown off, Madam?'

'(Loudly) £85? That's the charge for watching *Anal Intrusion 4* last night in your room.'

'I'm Peter, your concierge. I'm available throughout the night for room service, maintenance and joining in any sexual activity.'

'Every room has tea, coffee and freebasing facilities.'

'Are you with the Pneumatic Drillers' convention?'

'We're a bit overbooked but I do have a camp bed in the stable…'

B. Y. O. HEROIN

82. DISCARDED CARDS FROM THE 'HAPPY FAMILIES' PACK

Mr Bash the Bishop
Mr Pole the Builder
Mr Pissed the Pilot
Mr Trafficker the Lorry Driver
Mr Subsidy the Farmer
Mr Racist the Policeman
Mr C*nt the Estate Agent
Mr Crook the Lawyer
Mr Rich the Dentist
Mr Botch the Plasterer
Mr Doze the Lorry Driver
Mr Nancy the Air Steward
Mr Eurosceptic the Grocer
Mr Bent the Politician
Mr Corpse the Soldier
Mr Bigot the Van Driver
Mr Negligent the Electrician
Mrs Sexual Harassment Suit the Businesswoman
Mr Reckless the Bus Driver
Mr Profligate the Bank Manager
Miss Symptoms the Doctor
Mrs Inane the Hairdresser
Miss Drugs Test the Athlete
Mr Paedo the PE teacher
Mr Cowboy the Carpenter
Mr Prick the PR

83. LINES YOU'D NEVER SEE IN A JAMES BOND BOOK (Part 2)

'No, Mr Bond, I expect you to shit yourself.'

'James, he's using the diamonds to divert a giant laser onto New York from outer space.' Bond took the bottle out of M's shaking hand and helped her off the floor into bed.

'Now pay attention 007, this looks like an ordinary suitcase, but if you push this button, a handle comes out and you can wheel it.'

Bond left the casino. He always knew when he was tired, because he tended to nod off and piss himself.

Bond shut the door, locked it and with a tired sigh sat down on the bed. He took out his mascara and began to apply it.

Bond slid out of her and, checking she was asleep, noiselessly wiped his cock on the curtains.

'Flush, you bastard,' said Bond coldly, but the floater just stared back at him from the bowl.

'M should stand for Minge,' Bond said as he went down on her.

He was an educated man from a great family, a man of sophisticated tastes at the top of his profession and yet, as he began his task, the thought nagged away at him: he was now no more than a mercenary, a blunt tool used by forces more powerful than himself for their own ends. The great things he might have done – could still do – would forever now be devalued. 'F**k it, think of the money!' said Sebastian Faulks.

PHOTO CREDITS

FRONT COVER, TITLE PAGES:	**MOCK THE WEEK GLOBE CREATED BY MOOV**
P8:	**SHUTTERSTOCK**
P20/21:	**iSTOCKPHOTO**
P28, 29, 146, 147:	**iSTOCKPHOTO**
P35:	**iSTOCKPHOTO**
P42:	**iSTOCKPHOTO**
P50, 51, 100, 101, 102, 103:	**iSTOCKPHOTO**
P52:	**SHUTTERSTOCK**
P62/63:	**iSTOCKPHOTO**
P70:	**SHUTTERSTOCK**
P74:	**SHUTTERSTOCK / iSTOCKPHOTO**
P94/95:	**SHUTTERSTOCK**
P104:	**SHUTTERSTOCK**
P107:	**SHUTTERSTOCK**
P110:	**CORBIS / iSTOCKPHOTO**
P122:	**SHUTTERSTOCK**
P130, 144, 145:	**iSTOCKPHOTO**
P132/133:	**iSTOCKPHOTO**
P151:	**SHUTTERSTOCK**
P157:	**SHUTTERSTOCK**